Level F

Word Wisdom

Vocabulary for Listening, Speaking, Reading, and Writing

Author
Jerry Zutell, Ph.D.
The Ohio State University

Credits: Located on last page of book

ISBN: 0-7367-2450-8   Copyright © 2005 Zaner-Bloser, Inc.

Zaner-Bloser, Inc., P.O. Box 16764, Columbus, Ohio 43216-6764 (1-800-421-3018)
www.zaner-bloser.com

A ZB Language Arts Program

Contents

**9 UNIT THEME
Good and Bad 182**

PART 1 Context Clues

Context Clues

for Word Wisdom

A Great Speaker:
Dr. Martin Luther King, Jr.

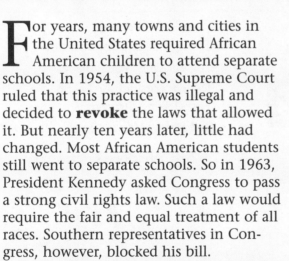

You spend most of your day listening to the people around you. But you don't just listen. You also speak, and people listen to you. Speakers can have a powerful effect on listeners. They can even change the world. One such speaker was Martin Luther King, Jr. Read this essay about a speech he gave on August 28, 1963.

For years, many towns and cities in the United States required African American children to attend separate schools. In 1954, the U.S. Supreme Court ruled that this practice was illegal and decided to **revoke** the laws that allowed it. But nearly ten years later, little had changed. Most African American students still went to separate schools. So in 1963, President Kennedy asked Congress to pass a strong civil rights law. Such a law would require the fair and equal treatment of all races. Southern representatives in Congress, however, blocked his bill.

Civil rights groups decided to hold a huge rally in Washington, D.C., to speak out in support of the new law. On August 28, 1963, more than 250,000 people from every part of the United States traveled to the nation's capital. Actors, folk singers, and other **advocates** of civil rights spoke to this huge crowd. Radio and television carried their words to millions. But it was the **eloquent** words that Reverend Martin Luther King, Jr., used to preach his message that will always be remembered.

Few speeches in American history have been as moving and **persuasive** as King's words were that day. He had planned a rather general speech on the evils and injustices of racism, but listeners called out for more. In a soft voice **audible** only to those on the speakers' platform, someone said, "Tell them about your dream." King's **response** was a speech that many consider a turning point in the civil rights movement. Standing in front of the Lincoln Memorial, King expressed his hope for a nation free of hate by repeating the words "I have a dream." That **refrain** contains some of the most memorable words in American history. Each time he referred to his dream, his words grew louder. When the **volume** of his voice peaked, King challenged Americans to live up to the American ideal: "We hold these truths to be self-evident, that all men are created equal." King's words were heard not only in Washington, D.C. They **resounded** through the entire nation. King's **oration** opened the nation's eyes to racial injustices as they had never been before. A year later, a civil rights law was passed.

Communication

Context Clues Strategy

Look for Objects or Ideas Related to the Word

EXAMPLE: Descriptive words, volume, and repetition helped the speaker *clarify* his message.

CLUE: The words *descriptive words, volume,* and *repetition* are related to the word *clarify* and help explain its meaning.

One way to understand the meanings of new words is to use context. The way new words are used with other words can give you clues to their meanings. Here are the steps for using context clues to understand the word *revoke* from the essay on page 6.

Read the sentence with the unknown word and some of the sentences around it.

*For years, many towns and cities in the United States required African American children to attend separate schools. In 1954, the U.S. Supreme Court ruled that this practice was illegal and decided to **revoke** the laws that allowed it.*

Look for context clues to the word's meaning. What **Objects or Ideas Related to the Word** can you find?

The words *illegal* and *revoke* are related. The word *illegal* means that separate schools were against the law. That's why the Supreme Court decided to revoke the laws that allowed this practice.

Think about the context clues and other information you may already know.

The Supreme Court can change or even throw out a law. If the court found a law to be illegal, it would probably use that power.

Predict a meaning for the word.

The Supreme Court must have thrown out or canceled laws that allowed separate schools. The word *revoke* must mean "to cancel" or "to throw out."

Check your Word Wisdom Dictionary to be sure of the meaning.

The word *revoke* means "to cancel or put an end to."

Practice the Strategy   Two of the boldfaced words from the essay on page 6 are listed below. Using the context clues strategy on page 7, follow these steps to figure out the meanings of these words.

eloquent

Read the sentence that uses the word *eloquent* and some of the sentences around it.

Look for context clues to the word's meaning. What **Objects or Ideas Related to the Word** can you find?

_____

Think about the context clues. What other helpful information do you know?

_____

Predict a meaning for the word *eloquent*.

_____

Check your Word Wisdom Dictionary to be sure of the meaning of the word *eloquent*. Which of the meanings for the word *eloquent* fits the context?

_____

audible

Read the sentence that uses the word *audible* and some of the sentences around it.

Look for context clues to the word's meaning. What **Objects or Ideas Related to the Word** can you find?

_____

Think about the context clues. What other helpful information do you know?

_____

Predict a meaning for the word *audible*.

_____

Check your dictionary to be sure of the meaning of the word *audible*. Write the definition here.

_____

✔ revoke
advocate
✔ eloquent
persuasive
✔ audible
response
refrain
volume
resound
oration

Use Context Clues You have been introduced to three vocabulary words from the essay about Dr. Martin Luther King. Those words are checked off in the Word List here. Under "Vocabulary Word" below, write the other seven words from the Word List. Predict a meaning for each word under "Your Prediction." Then check the meanings in the Word Wisdom Dictionary. Write the definition under "Dictionary Says."

	Vocabulary Word	Your Prediction	Dictionary Says
1			
2			
3			
4			
5			
6			
7			

Process the Meanings

WORD LIST

revoke

advocate

eloquent

persuasive

audible

response

refrain

volume

resound

oration

Use the Words Correctly in Writing Rewrite each sentence in your own words. Include the word in parentheses in your sentence. You may need to add an ending to the word.

1 Stan lost so many books that the librarian canceled his library card. (revoke)

_____

2 Many students are in favor of more time for after-school sports. (advocate)

_____

3 Thanks to his lawyer's arguments, the guilty man received a light sentence. (eloquent)

_____

4 Some of the clever commercials on television really convince people to buy things. (persuasive)

_____

5 The child spoke so softly that people nearby couldn't hear her words. (audible)

_____

6 I liked your clear answer to my last question. (response)

_____

7 After hearing parts of the song several times, I started to sing along. (refrain)

_____

8 There must be something wrong with the CD player because I can hardly hear the song. (volume)

_____

9 When the home team scored the winning touchdown, cheers could be heard all through the town. (resound)

_____

10 We had hoped for a lively debate, but instead we heard one long, boring speech after another. (oration)

_____

Apply What You've Learned

Relate the Meanings   Answer the questions or follow the directions.

1 What is one privilege that your teacher or school principal could **revoke**?

_____

2 What would an **advocate** for the environment want you to do?

_____

3 Who would have to be an **eloquent** speaker—an acrobat or a politician?

_____

4 What kind of **response** would you give on an essay test?

_____

5 Name some people who must be **persuasive** in order to be successful.

_____

6 What is **audible** to you as you walk through the halls at school?

_____

7 What is the **refrain** of the song often sung at birthday parties?

_____

8 What happens when you turn down the **volume** on a radio?

_____

9 Tell about a time when the voices of you and your classmates **resound** throughout the room.

_____

10 Name an event where you would expect an **oration**.

_____

 Write It!   Write a story about one of the sentences above. Use as many words from the Word List on page 10 as you can.

PART 2

Latin Roots

for Word Wisdom

Speak Up!

Become a Stronger Speaker

Do you hate to speak in public? Do you get nervous just standing up in front of a crowd? If so, you are like most people—public speaking is one of the most common phobias in the world.

Like most people, you probably would rather do anything than speak in front of a **convocation** of class-mates and staff at school. You may even avoid **auditions** for school plays. However, you—and all the people like you—could master the art of **elocution** and become a stronger speaker by following the simple guidelines below.

1. Know your audience. Know their interests and the experiences you share with them. To connect with your audience, you might **evoke** memories of these shared experiences. You also should know whether they prefer formal language or more **colloquial** expressions.

2. Have a clear goal in mind. Decide whether you will inform, persuade, or entertain your audience. Choose a topic that really interests you and your audience. Decide on two or three main points and include only details that relate to those points.

3. Understand how your audience learns best. For example, do your class-mates like to receive information from pictures and charts, or do they prefer to sit and listen to a speaker? Many audiences like a combined visual and auditory presentation. Displaying visual aids during your speech tends to make it clearer and more interesting. The aids also give your audience something to look at, besides you. In addition, writing your main points on charts or overheads can help you remember what you want to say.

4. Outline your speech. Think of an opening that will grab your audience's attention. For example, you might begin with a startling statistic or a meaningful quotation. You could also begin with a comment that **provokes** the audience to sit up and say, "Wait a minute!" You might tell a joke, but be careful not to offend anyone.

5. Make note cards with your main points and details. Number the cards to make it easy to keep them in order. Then practice your speech several times, but do not read it. Decide where to vary your presentation by speaking louder, softer, slower, or faster. Decide when to use your visual aids. As you practice, pretend to make eye contact with different members of your audience.

6. Now it's time to **invoke** the help of your family or friends. Ask them to listen to your speech and suggest ways to improve your performance. You can also make an **audio** or video recording of your speech in order to evaluate your presentation.

By following these guidelines, you will strengthen your speaking skills. You might even decide to choose public speaking as a **vocation**!

Practice the Context Clues Strategy Two of the boldfaced words from the selection on page 12 appear below. Use the context clues strategy that you learned in Part 1 on page 7 to figure out the meanings of these words.

convocation

Read the sentence that uses the word *convocation* and some of the sentences around it.

Look for context clues to the word's meaning. What **Objects or Ideas Related to the Word** can you find?

_____

Think about the context clues. What other helpful information do you know?

_____

Predict a meaning for the word *convocation*.

_____

Check your Word Wisdom Dictionary to be sure of the meaning of the word *convocation*. Write the meaning here.

_____

invoke

Read the sentence that uses the word *invoke* and some of the sentences around it.

Look for context clues to the word's meaning. What **Objects or Ideas Related to the Word** can you find?

_____

Think about the context clues. What other helpful information do you know?

_____

Predict a meaning for the word *invoke*.

_____

Check your Word Wisdom Dictionary to be sure of the meaning of the word *invoke*. Which of the meanings for the word *invoke* fits the context?

Unlock the Meanings

Many English words are made from Latin roots. Knowing the meanings of roots will help you unlock the meaning of many unknown words. Several words you studied in Part 1 have Latin roots. Each root is related to communication.

Latin Root: **voc, vok**
meaning: voice, call
English word: *revoke*
meaning: to cancel or put an end to

Latin Root: **audi**
meaning: hear
English word: *audible*
meaning: loud enough to be heard

Latin Root: **loqu, locu**
meaning: speak
English word: *eloquent*
meaning: powerful or moving

WORD LIST

convocation
audition
elocution
evoke
colloquial
auditory
provoke
invoke
audio
vocation

Categorize by Roots Find these roots in the Word List. Then write each word in the correct part of the tree. Think of other words you know that come from the same Latin roots. Write them in the correct parts of the tree.

Latin Root: **voc, vok**

_____

_____

_____

_____

_____

Latin Root: **audi**

_____

_____

_____

_____

_____

Latin Root: **loqu, locu**

_____

_____

_____

_____

_____

Communication

Prefix	Meaning
co-, con-	together
in-	not
pro-	in favor of
e-	from

Example

con- (together) + **voc** (call) + **-ation** (noun) = **convocation**

Practice Using Roots and Prefixes   Circle any roots and prefixes you find in the boldfaced words below. Use context clues, roots, and prefixes to write the meaning of the word. Check your definitions in the dictionary.

1 A **convocation** of elected officials discussed the need for new taxes.

_____

2 The **audition** allows each actor ten minutes in front of the director.

_____

3 The speaker had such good **elocution** that everyone understood her.

_____

4 I knew my criticism of her friend would **provoke** an argument.

_____

5 The song on the radio **evoked** memories of last summer's vacation.

_____

6 The witness will **invoke** his rights under the Constitution.

_____

7 She always knew she had a **vocation** for social work.

_____

8 Please turn down the **audio control** on the television.

_____

9 The manager refused to read the letter of application that began with the **colloquial** expression "How's it going?"

_____

10 The salesperson said that the new stereo equipment would give me the **auditory** experience of a lifetime.

_____

WORD LIST

- convocation
- audition
- elocution
- evoke
- colloquial
- auditory
- provoke
- invoke
- audio
- vocation

Choose the Correct Word Write the word from the Word List that completes each sentence.

1 The _____ part of the concert was broadcast on radio as well as on television.

2 A(n) _____ will be held on Thursday for singers and dancers in the new musical.

3 Just because you like wearing a white jacket doesn't mean you have a _____ for medicine.

4 The gymnasium was decorated with palm trees to _____ the feeling of a tropical island.

5 Students from all over the state attended the recent _____ on physical fitness.

6 Because of the riots, the governor had to _____ her authority to use the National Guard to restore law and order.

7 After seeing the results of the hearing tests, the doctor suspected his patient had damaged his _____ nerve.

8 She took a special class in _____ to help her pronounce words more clearly.

9 Mark Twain's characters use many colorful _____ expressions.

10 No matter what his neighbor said, Jerry would not let his words _____ him into starting a fight.

Demonstrate Word Knowledge Answer the questions or follow the directions.

1 What is the difference between a **vacation** and a **vocation**?

_____

_____

2 Write a **colloquial** way of saying "good-bye."

_____

_____

3 What would you find in the **audio** department of a large store?

_____

_____

4 Why are **auditions** held before instead of after a play opens?

_____

_____

5 Why might someone call a **convocation**?

_____

_____

Solve the Riddle Write a word from the Word List on page 16 for each clue. The underlined words will help you.

_____ **6** It's a way of <u>calling to mind</u> something else.

_____ **7** This is the type of <u>speech</u> you use with a friend.

_____ **8** I hear people <u>showing off their talent</u>.

_____ **9** This four-syllable word is related in meaning to <u>diction</u>.

_____ **10** What else would you call the nerve in your body that lets you <u>hear</u>?

Speak It! Give a talk about the importance of communication. Use as many words from Part 2 as you can.

PART 3 Reference Skills

for Word Wisdom

Chief Joseph:
Speak the Truth

"It does not require many words to speak the truth."

—Chief Joseph

These wise words were **uttered** by Chief Joseph (1840–1904). He was the powerful and respected leader of the Native American Nez Perce nation.

The Nez Perce were a peaceful people. They helped Lewis and Clark survive their expedition across the Northwest. At that time, Nez Perce land spread from Idaho to northern Washington. After the expedition passed through, the Nez Perce had good relations with other explorers and settlers. In 1855, Chief Joseph's father, Old Joseph, signed a treaty with the United States government. The treaty allowed the Nez Perce to keep much of the land where they had lived for centuries.

Unfortunately, in 1863, gold was discovered on this land. The government decided to "take back" most of the land—almost six million acres. Federal officials created a second treaty. This treaty reduced the land owned by the Nez Perce to one tenth of its size. They were left with only a small reservation in Idaho.

Old Joseph **renounced** this treaty. He insisted that he had never agreed to it. Young Joseph became chief in 1877. The government tried to force the Nez Perce to move from their homeland in Oregon to the reservation in Idaho. Chief Joseph refused to move his people. After a long and bloody battle, the Nez Perce were greatly outnumbered. They finally surrendered. The government sent many of them to live on a reservation in what is now Oklahoma. Many died there of sickness and starvation.

At great risk to himself, Chief Joseph did not remain **mute**. He attempted to set up a **discourse** with the government about his people's land. Having lived with a Christian missionary as a child, the chief spoke **fluent** English. He was not a **verbose** man, but when he spoke, people listened. He was able to **verbalize** the frustrations of many Native American nations as they lost their lands. They knew their entire cultures were being threatened.

Chief Joseph **inquired** many times about ways for his people to regain more of their traditional lands. He even traveled to Washington, D.C., to talk to President Rutherford B. Hayes. Still, his requests fell on deaf ears. In 1885, he and his followers were sent to a reservation in Washington State. It was not even on Nez Perce land. They were kept separate from their people in Idaho and from their homeland in Oregon.

Discouraged, Chief Joseph died several years later. People say that he died of a broken heart. Perhaps they **exaggerate,** but perhaps not.

People today recognize the wisdom in the chief's words. His **lucid** thoughts relate to our daily lives. It still does not require many words to speak the truth.

Practice the Context Clues Strategy Two of the boldfaced words from the selection on page 18 appear below. Use the context clues strategy you learned in Part 1 on page 7 to figure out the meanings of these words.

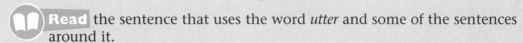

utter

📖 **Read** the sentence that uses the word *utter* and some of the sentences around it.

🔍 **Look** for context clues to the word's meaning. What **Objects or Ideas Related to the Word** can you find?

_____

💡 **Think** about the context clues. What other helpful information do you know?

_____

➡️ **Predict** a meaning for the word *utter*.

_____

✔️ **Check** your Word Wisdom Dictionary to be sure of the meaning of the word *utter*. Which of the meanings for the word *utter* fits the context?

_____

renounce

📖 **Read** the sentence that uses the word *renounce* and some of the sentences around it.

🔍 **Look** for context clues to the word's meaning. What **Objects or Ideas Related to the Word** can you find?

_____

💡 **Think** about the context clues. What other helpful information do you know?

_____

➡️ **Predict** a meaning for the word *renounce*.

_____

✔️ **Check** your Word Wisdom Dictionary to be sure of the meaning of the word *renounce*. Write the definition here.

_____

🔒 Unlock the Meanings

Idioms and Special Dictionaries An *idiom* is an expression with a special meaning. It cannot be understood from the meaning of each word. Look again at the essay on page 6. Read the first sentence of paragraph 2. Can you find the idiom? Here's that sentence: *Civil rights groups decided to hold a huge rally in Washington, D.C., to speak out in support of the new law.* The words *speak out* form an idiom. When used in this way, they mean "to say something for or against a person or idea."

You can find the meanings of idioms in a specialized dictionary, such as *A Dictionary of American Idioms.*

Find Idioms in a Special Dictionary Here are some common idioms about communication. Choose a word from the Word List on page 21 that relates to each idiom. Write it on the line. Check your answers in a dictionary that contains idioms.

1 Stan often blows things out of proportion.

_____

2 She tried to speak to the crowd, but the cat got her tongue.

_____

3 Your explanation was crystal clear.

_____

4 He could talk your head off!

_____

5 Can you put that into words?

_____

Find the Meaning

1. Use context clues.
2. Look for a familiar root, prefix, or suffix.
3. If the context or a word part doesn't help, check the dictionary.

WORD LIST

utter
renounce
mute
discourse
fluent
verbose
verbalize
inquire
exaggerate
lucid

Define the Words Follow the steps above to write the meaning of each boldfaced word. Then write 1, 2, or 3 to show which steps you used.

1 I couldn't find the music room, so I **inquired** about directions.

_____

2 Mom and I had a long **discourse** on my opportunities after graduation.

_____

3 The gymnasium walls could not **mute** the cheers of the crowd.

_____

4 The actor's **verbose** acceptance speech lasted ten minutes.

_____

5 George Washington **renounced** any attempts to make him king.

_____

6 Many authors are able to **verbalize** what other people feel.

_____

7 When asked how he pleaded, the defendant quietly **uttered** "guilty."

_____

8 Thanks to the teacher's **lucid** explanation, I finally understood math.

_____

9 In his resume, the applicant tried to **exaggerate** his job skills.

_____

10 I know enough French to get by, but I am not **fluent** in the language.

_____

Process the Meanings

WORD LIST

- utter
- renounce
- mute
- discourse
- fluent
- verbose
- verbalize
- inquire
- exaggerate
- lucid

Choose the Correct Word   Write the word from the Word List that completes each sentence. You may need to add an ending to some words.

1 At graduation, the speaker launched into a long _____ on the importance of education.

2 Only a brilliant scientist could give such a _____ explanation of how the satellite works.

3 I'll never believe any of Jerry's wild stories, since he always _____ things.

4 The defendant's lawyer _____ the jury's verdict and demanded a new trial.

5 When I do my homework, I need earplugs to _____ the sound of my brother's drums.

6 I know which team we are playing, but I need to _____ about the game's starting time.

7 After spending a year in Spain, I became quite _____ in Spanish.

8 It is often difficult to _____ one's grief after a terrible tragedy.

9 Be very, very quiet; don't _____ a sound.

10 To keep the speeches from becoming too _____, a time limit of five minutes was given.

Find the Synonyms Match each vocabulary word with its synonym. Write the synonym on the line.

Vocabulary Word	Synonym
1 lucid _____	wordy
2 exaggerate _____	reject
3 verbose _____	silent
4 utter _____	clear
5 renounce _____	say
6 mute _____	overstate
7 inquire _____	speech
8 verbalize _____	flowing
9 discourse _____	ask
10 fluent _____	express

Write It! Use a special dictionary to get ideas to write three of your own idioms.

Review

for Word Wisdom

What's the Root? Study each word in the list. If the word has one of the roots shown in the diagram, write the word in the space with the root. Then draw a line through the word on the list.

WORD LIST

- revoke
- advocate
- eloquent
- persuasive
- audible
- response
- refrain
- volume
- resound
- oration
- convocation
- audition
- elocution
- evoke
- colloquial
- auditory
- provoke
- invoke
- audio
- vocation
- utter
- renounce
- mute
- discourse
- fluent
- verbose
- verbalize
- inquire
- exaggerate
- lucid

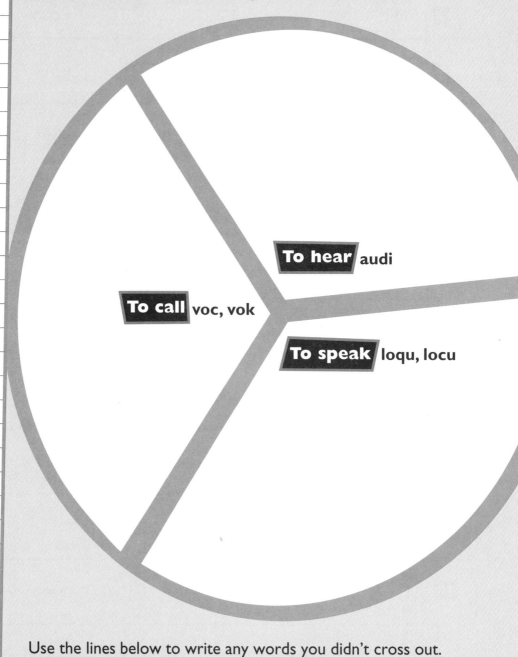

To hear / audi

To call / voc, vok

To speak / loqu, locu

Use the lines below to write any words you didn't cross out.

_____

_____

_____

Choose the Correct Word   Write a word from the list on page 24 to complete each statement. You may need to add an ending to the word.

1 The speaker's words were not _____ in the last row.

2 The soloist asked us to join her in singing the _____.

3 A(n) _____ for the homeless created more shelters.

4 The witness chose to _____ his right not to testify.

5 Our teacher chose her words carefully to _____ her thoughts about what we should do.

6 The candidate's _____ during the debate won her many votes.

7 Bad drivers will have their licenses _____.

8 The _____ system in our television sounds realistic.

9 A clap of thunder _____ through the hills.

10 I _____ about prices before spending my money.

Check the Meaning   If the underlined word is used correctly, write **C**. If the underlined word is used incorrectly, write **I**.

_____ **11** Henry made a mistake in <u>audition</u> when he added the numbers.

_____ **12** She lost my vote when she didn't give <u>lucid</u> answers.

_____ **13** Lincoln's <u>oration</u> at Gettysburg lasted only ten minutes.

_____ **14** In <u>colloquial</u> America, people farmed or practiced simple trades.

_____ **15** I wasn't listening earlier, so please <u>renounce</u> the message.

_____ **16** Experts claim that loud music damages a listener's <u>auditory</u> nerve.

_____ **17** The <u>discourse</u> for the race led runners through town.

_____ **18** The restaurant was so <u>eloquent</u> that the waiters wore tuxedos.

_____ **19** The artist uses dark colors to <u>evoke</u> sadness in his paintings.

_____ **20** Please <u>mute</u> the television so I can hear what you are saying.

Taking Vocabulary Tests

TEST-TAKING STRATEGY

Some vocabulary tests ask you to choose the meaning of a word in a short phrase. Often one or more incorrect choices will make sense, but don't let this trick you into marking the wrong answer. You must think about the meaning of the word. Then eliminate the answers you know are wrong and make your choice. Each of the answer choices makes sense in the sample below, but only one has the same meaning as the underlined word.

Sample:

a <u>favorite</u> teacher
- ○ smart
- ● best-liked
- ○ creative
- ○ pleasant

Practice Test Fill in the circle for the word or words that have the SAME or ALMOST THE SAME meaning as the underlined word.

1 the <u>convocation</u> of experts
- ○ opinion
- ○ gathering
- ○ argument
- ○ pastime

2 <u>provoke</u> a fight
- ○ cause
- ○ delay
- ○ cancel
- ○ win

3 <u>exaggerate</u> the results
- ○ deliver
- ○ change
- ○ hide
- ○ enlarge

4 <u>utter</u> a remark
- ○ deny
- ○ state
- ○ call back
- ○ read

5 a correct <u>response</u>
- ○ attempt
- ○ order
- ○ answer
- ○ meeting

6 increase the <u>volume</u>
- ○ audience
- ○ length
- ○ movement
- ○ loudness

7 a <u>vocation</u> to teach
- ○ topic
- ○ calling
- ○ story
- ○ speech pattern

8 a <u>fluent</u> speaker
- ○ foreign
- ○ exciting
- ○ graceful
- ○ clever

9 a <u>verbose</u> answer
- ○ confusing
- ○ simple
- ○ wordy
- ○ quiet

10 a <u>persuasive</u> speech
- ○ convincing
- ○ frightening
- ○ long
- ○ rude

Build New Words

Use Suffixes The suffix *-ation* makes a word a noun. The suffix *-ative* makes a word an adjective. Use these suffixes to make new words from *invoke, evoke, provoke, exaggerate,* and *verbalize*. You will need to change the spellings. Then write the meanings of the new words and check your Word Wisdom Dictionary to make sure your definition is correct.

Word	+ Suffix	= New Word	Meaning
invoke			
evoke			
provoke			
exaggerate			
verbalize			

Speak It! Pretend you are running for a political office. Give a speech to convince your classmates to vote for you. Use as many words from this Communication unit as you can.

Context Clues

for Word Wisdom

Using Our Senses:
The Nose Knows

With its trillions of cells and complex processes, the human body is an engineering and communication marvel. Doctors and scientists have tried for years to figure out how the body works and what to do when it doesn't. Read this article to uncover some of the secrets of our sense of smell.

Have you ever tried to describe a favorite smell to someone who hasn't experienced it? Imagine that a delicious cake is baking in the oven. It's hard to find words to capture the vanilla and cinnamon fragrance of that warm kitchen. What if you want to tell about the pine and earthy odor of a forest? People end up comparing the smell to something else or describing how it makes them feel. Surprisingly, the functions and activities, or the **physiology,** of this sense are fairly simple and direct.

The sense of smell is part of **respiration,** which is the physical process of breathing. Inhaling and exhaling, we live in a constant stream of odors. These odors are molecules of evaporated chemicals that float in the air.

Normal breathing through the nose allows us to pick up most smells. A sharp sniff sends even more molecules into the nasal cavity behind the bridge of the nose. This cavity is lined with a thin layer of watery material called mucus and also with tiny hair-like projections. On these projections are highly **sensitive** receptor cells, which are easily stimulated. These cells fire millions of impulses to the brain's smell center. This is why, when you have **symptoms,** or signs, of a cold, you may lose your sense of smell. When the body produces too much mucus, the nerve impulses are slowed or stopped.

Different parts of the brain's smell center are sensitive to different odors. When some nerve endings are stimulated, others aren't. The specific combination is like a code that the brain interprets. The average person can detect more than ten thousand different odors, from the **benign,** or harmless, scent of baby powder to the stench of rotten eggs.

Smell is probably the most direct of the senses. Other sense organs also send messages to the brain, but often these must pass through other organs along the way. This means that smell is one of our stronger, more **potent,** senses. A **corps,** or body, of researchers has studied how fragrance affects people. These scientists tested people who have a strong **constitution** and a healthy medical history. One finding is that the smell of spiced apples reduces blood pressure. Cloves and rosemary make test subjects more alert. Thyme and peppermint **rejuvenate** tired workers. One experiment even showed that the scent of chamomile reduced **inflammation** and contributed to the healing of infections. Our sense of smell affects all aspects of our health and well-being.

Context Clues Strategy

Look for Definitions, Descriptions, or Synonyms

EXAMPLE: The term *fitness* means good health or good physical condition.

CLUE: The words *term* and *means* let you know that the word *fitness* is being defined in the sentence.

Here are the steps for using this context clues strategy to figure out the meaning of the word *respiration*, which appeared in the article about the sense of smell.

Read the sentence with the unknown word and some of the sentences around it.

- - - - -

The sense of smell is part of **respiration**, *which is the physical process of breathing.*

Look for context clues. What **Definitions, Descriptions, or Synonyms** can you find?

- - - - -

The words *which is* are clues that the word *respiration* is being defined in the same sentence. The words *the physical process of breathing* provide the definition.

Think about the context clues and other helpful information you already know.

- - - - -

The nose and mouth are both used in breathing.

Predict a meaning for the word.

- - - - -

The word *respiration* must mean "breathing."

Check your Word Wisdom Dictionary to see how it defines the word.

- - - - -

The word *respiration* means "the process of breathing."

🔑 Unlock the Meanings

Practice the Strategy   Here are two of the boldfaced words from the article on page 28. Use the context clues strategy on page 29 to figure out the meaning of each word.

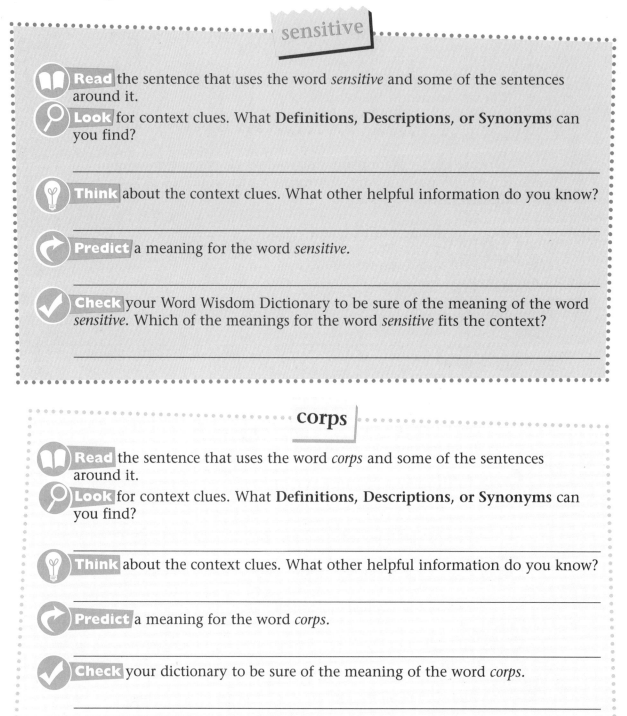

sensitive

📖 **Read** the sentence that uses the word *sensitive* and some of the sentences around it.

🔍 **Look** for context clues. What **Definitions, Descriptions, or Synonyms** can you find?

_____

💡 **Think** about the context clues. What other helpful information do you know?

_____

➡ **Predict** a meaning for the word *sensitive*.

_____

✔ **Check** your Word Wisdom Dictionary to be sure of the meaning of the word *sensitive*. Which of the meanings for the word *sensitive* fits the context?

_____

corps

📖 **Read** the sentence that uses the word *corps* and some of the sentences around it.

🔍 **Look** for context clues. What **Definitions, Descriptions, or Synonyms** can you find?

_____

💡 **Think** about the context clues. What other helpful information do you know?

_____

➡ **Predict** a meaning for the word *corps*.

_____

✔ **Check** your dictionary to be sure of the meaning of the word *corps*.

_____

physiology
✔ respiration
✔ sensitive
symptom
benign
potent
✔ corps
constitution
rejuvenate
inflammation

Use Context Clues   You have been introduced to three vocabulary words from the article on page 28. Those words are checked off in the Word List here. Under "Vocabulary Word" below, write the other seven words from the Word List. Use context clues to predict a meaning for each word under "Your Prediction." Then check the meanings in the Word Wisdom Dictionary. Write the definition under "Dictionary Says."

	Vocabulary Word	Your Prediction	Dictionary Says
1			
2			
3			
4			
5			
6			
7			

Process the Meanings

WORD LIST

- physiology
- respiration
- sensitive
- symptom
- benign
- potent
- corps
- constitution
- rejuvenate
- inflammation

Choose the Correct Word for the Context Complete each sentence with the word from the Word List that best fits the context.

1 Fortunately, the growth on our dog's leg was _____; within two days, he was chasing his ball as if he hadn't had surgery.

2 People with asthma may experience a feeling of tightness in the chest and labored _____.

3 After a morning of planting and weeding, Mr. Luz takes a hot shower and a nap to _____ himself.

4 Liza can soak her toe in cold water to reduce the pain and puffiness of the _____.

5 The three-dimensional color diagrams helped us understand the _____ of the eye.

6 First-year medical students have a tendency to experience every _____ of diseases that they study.

7 Antibiotics, such as penicillin and streptomycin, are _____ defenders against infectious diseases.

8 Many charities depend on a _____ of volunteers to carry out their work.

9 Mason's skin is highly _____ to wool; whenever he wears it, he gets a terrible rash.

10 Granddad attributes his strong _____ to a life of hard work and a daily swim in the cool ocean water.

Apply What You've Learned

Use the Words Correctly Use what you've learned about the boldfaced words to complete the following sentences.

1 A person might improve his or her **constitution** by _____

_____

2 Someone who is **sensitive** to the feelings of others might _____

_____

3 You might **rejuvenate** the enthusiasm of club members by _____

_____

4 A medical technician might give artificial **respiration** to someone who

_____

5 _____ usually has a **benign** climate in the winter.

6 A person interested in _____

might read a book about its **physiology**.

7 One common **symptom** of a stomach virus is _____

_____

8 Is this pill **potent** enough to _____

_____

9 A member of the drum and bugle **corps** might _____

_____

10 One way to reduce minor **inflammation** is _____

_____

Write It! Helen Keller once said, "Smell is a potent wizard that transports us across thousands of miles and all the years we have lived. . . . Even as I think of smells, my nose is full of scents that start [to] awake sweet memories of summers gone and ripening fields far away." Write about an experience that you associate with a particular smell. Use as many words as you can from the Word List on page 32.

PART 2

Latin Roots

for Word Wisdom

The Body Reacts:
Allergy Alert

Up to fifty million Americans have some type of allergy. Allergies can be a small inconvenience, or they can rule your life. The more you know about them, the better you can understand how they affect you or others.

Allergies occur when the body thinks a certain substance is harmful. The immune system releases chemicals to fight it off. These chemicals then trigger allergic symptoms. So, you can say that allergic reactions are caused by an overactive immune system. If you don't have allergies, a day at the park might be a pleasant **sensory** experience. If you do have allergies, however, an attack can give you the unpleasant **sensation** of suffocating. The tissues in your nose and windpipe suddenly swell. They begin to produce excess mucus that clogs your breathing passages. As a result, you might feel as if you are wearing a tight **corset** that prevents you from drawing a breath.

People can be allergic to things they breathe, things they eat, or things they touch. Millions of people are allergic to pollen and dust particles in the air. The most common food allergy among infants and children is cow's milk. Some people have an allergic reaction when they touch pets. Some are even allergic to things they smell, such as perfume or laundry detergent.

A serious allergy attack can threaten your survival. An allergy to peanuts, for example, can have a total **corporal** effect, which means that many organs can be involved. The result can be fatal. An attack of respiratory allergies might not be fatal, but it can be frightening. Struggling to breathe, you might feel as if you are about to **expire**. Infants might **aspirate** mucus into their lungs. To avoid becoming a **corpse,** some allergy sufferers carry inhalers. They are filled with medicine that helps reduce swelling in the airways of the lungs. This **sensible** approach prevents much suffering and misery.

Most allergy sufferers try to avoid things that set off their allergic reactions. If the problem cannot be avoided, injections may be the answer. Some people get a shot once a week or every two weeks. The shot contains small amounts of the substance to which they are allergic. The dose is increased slightly each time. This treatment **desensitizes** the body, which means the body has less reaction to the substance. After a while, a shot once a month is enough to prevent reactions. These shots might continue for three years, five years, or even longer.

If you think you have an allergy, don't worry or **perspire**. Talk to your parents. They might take you to your family doctor or a specialist. He or she can test your reaction to different substances. If you do have an allergy, many effective treatments can help you cope with it. You can breathe easier just knowing that.

Practice the Context Clues Strategy Here are two of the boldfaced words from the essay on page 34. Use the context clues strategy you learned in Part 1 on page 29 to figure out the meanings of these words.

desensitizes

Read the sentence that uses the word *desensitizes* and some of the sentences around it.

Look for context clues to the word's meaning. What **Definitions, Descriptions, or Synonyms** can you find?

_____

_____

Think about the context clues. What other information do you know?

_____

Predict a meaning for the word *desensitize*.

_____

Check your Word Wisdom Dictionary to be sure of the meaning of the word *desensitize*. Write the definition here.

_____

corporal

Read the sentence that uses the word *corporal* and some of the sentences around it.

Look for context clues to the word's meaning. What **Definitions, Descriptions, or Synonyms** can you find?

_____

Think about the context clues. What other information do you know?

_____

Predict a meaning for the word *corporal*.

_____

Check your Word Wisdom Dictionary to be sure of the meaning of the word *corporal*. Which of the meanings for the word *corporal* fits the context?

_____

🔒 Unlock the Meanings

Several words you studied in Part 1 have Latin roots. Knowing the meaning of these roots will help you unlock the meaning of many unfamiliar words. Each root below is related to the body.

Latin Root: **sens**	Latin Root: **spir**	Latin Root: **corp**
meaning: to feel	meaning: to breathe	meaning: body
English word: *sensitive*	English word: *respiration*	English word: *corps*
meaning: affected by external stimuli; easily irritated	meaning: the act of inhaling and exhaling; breathing	meaning: a body of people who act together

WORD LIST

- sensory
- sensation
- corset
- corporal
- expire
- aspirate
- corpse
- sensible
- desensitize
- perspire

Categorize by Roots Find these roots in the Word List. Write each word in the correct column. Two words come from these roots but are not spelled like these roots. Think of other words you know that come from the same Latin roots. Write each word in the correct column.

Latin Root: sens	Latin Root: spir	Latin Root: corp
_____	_____	_____
_____	_____	_____
_____	_____	_____
_____	_____	_____
_____	_____	_____

The Body

Prefix	Meaning
de-	reduce
ex-	without, not
per-	completely

Example

de- (reduce) + **sens** (to feel) + **-itize** (verb) = **desensitize**

Use Roots and Prefixes   Circle the root and any prefixes you find in the boldfaced words below. Use context clues, roots, and prefixes to write the meaning of the word. Check your definitions in the Word Wisdom Dictionary.

1 A person is said to **expire** when he or she takes a last breath.

_____

2 Doctors may **aspirate** a patient's airways to help the person breathe better.

_____

3 The unusual smells, tastes, and sounds made Glen's first visit to an Indian restaurant an exciting **sensory** experience.

_____

4 My great aunt wore a tight **corset** to make her waist look tiny.

_____

5 When a person **perspires**, sweat cools the body by evaporation.

_____

6 Many people who have allergies to grass get injections that **desensitize** them to pollen.

_____

7 By examining the **corpse,** the coroner determined how the man died.

_____

8 Slippers would not be the most **sensible** shoes to wear on a hike.

_____

9 Born with a **corporal** defect, young Lacey had two heart operations.

_____

10 Sam loves amusement park rides that give him the **sensation** of flying.

_____

Process the Meanings

WORD LIST

- sensory
- sensation
- corset
- corporal
- expire
- aspirate
- corpse
- sensible
- desensitize
- perspire

Choose the Correct Word   Write the word from the Word List that can replace the underlined word or group of words in each sentence. You will need to add an ending to a few words.

1 Kim lost all <u>feeling</u> in her left leg after sitting with it tucked underneath her for a half hour. _____

2 If you have never been to a rock concert, your first experience may be one of an overload <u>of the senses</u>. _____

3 In the past, <u>bodily</u> punishment was seen as a reasonable way to discipline prisoners. _____

4 Laughing while drinking a glass of juice, Jason <u>inhaled</u> the liquid <u>and began to cough.</u> _____

5 One way to <u>make</u> yourself <u>immune to</u> your greatest fears is to expose yourself to them little by little. _____

6 Tennis players who <u>sweat</u> a lot often wear headbands to keep the moisture out of their eyes. _____

7 The mystery was about who had placed the <u>dead body</u> in the creek. _____

8 At the bottom of the chart, the nurse wrote the time, 12:03 A.M., when the patient <u>took his last breath</u>. _____

9 One of the favorite babysitters in town, Michaela was <u>showing good judgment</u> for her age. _____

10 After back surgery, Julie wore a comfortable <u>undergarment that provided support</u> until she healed completely. _____

Demonstrate Word Knowledge Complete each of the following statements.

1 People tend to **perspire** when they _____

_____

2 A woman might wear a **corset** because _____

_____

3 A funeral director would pick up a **corpse** at a _____

_____

4 Some experts are concerned that children may be **desensitized** to violence

because _____

5 A doctor may have to **aspirate** a patient if _____

_____

6 A teacher who asks students to use **sensory** details in their writing wants

them to _____

7 Sometimes people need **corporal** replacements such as hips and knees

because _____

8 If you have the **sensation** of "butterflies in your stomach," you may be

feeling _____

9 A **sensible** diet would be one that is _____

_____

10 A stuffed animal could not **expire** because _____

_____

Speak It! Describe a time when you had "butterflies in your stomach." Why did you have them? When and how did they go away? Use as many words as you can from the Word List on page 38.

PART 3 Reference Skills

Take the Stairs: Stepping Up to Good Health

Every day, doctors tell their patients to exercise more—take a jog, lift weights, go for a swim. But how can you fit exercise into your busy day? Why is exercise so important?

People used to believe that exercise did more harm than good. Many people thought that exercise would only cause a bone **fracture** or a heart attack. Today, health experts urge all people to stay active. **Physical** activity helps people to build **stamina,** which allows them to enjoy activities without tiring.

Regular exercise also helps strengthen stomach and back muscles. These muscles are important in maintaining good **posture**. Good posture, in turn, helps avoid back pain and other **afflictions** that can keep people from being active.

Do people need to join a health club to exercise? Not at all! Instead, some health experts urge people to take advantage of a free exercise device—stairs. Climbing stairs requires lifting your body up against gravity. This effort helps strengthen your heart, muscles, and bones. People of all ages can benefit from taking the stairs more often.

Yet ninety-five percent of the people in one Baltimore study did not take the stairs. They chose to ride an escalator instead. Escalators, moving walkways, and automatic doors make life too easy for us. They allow us to avoid exercise without even realizing it.

Besides giving us strength, exercise can also keep us healthy. In a Harvard study of 11,000 men, those who climbed at least 20 flights of stairs a week had a 20 percent lower risk of stroke.

Physical activity helps us maintain our **vigor** as long as possible. Many of us can avoid becoming an **invalid** simply by exercising a little throughout the day. For example, at the National Institutes of Health in Maryland, employees are urged to take the stairs. Signs remind them of the benefits. For example, one sign reads, "Burn some stress, take the stairs."

Step aerobics, a popular form of exercise, requires going up and down a step thirty to sixty times a minute. An exercise machine called a stair climber provides this same form of exercise, but these machines are expensive.

Of course, people should check with their doctors before starting an exercise program. This is especially true for older people. Dizziness, **nausea,** shortness of breath, or joint pain can be signs of trouble.

You can start your own fitness program for free right now. Find a set of stairs. Take a deep breath, and then **exhale**. Now, climb those stairs! You can climb them once or as many times as possible. As you make stair climbing a regular part of your day, you will feel fitter and have more stamina. You will stand straighter and feel better. Even your **complexion** may improve! For sure, you will feel proud of the way you are taking care of your body.

Practice the Context Clues Strategy   Here are two of the boldfaced words from the essay on page 40. Use the context clues strategy you learned in Part 1 on page 29 to figure out the meanings of these words.

stamina

Read the sentence that uses the word *stamina* and some of the sentences around it.

Look for context clues to the word's meaning. What **Definitions, Descriptions, or Synonyms** can you find?

_____

Think about the context clues. What other information do you know?

_____

Predict a meaning for the word *stamina*.

_____

Check your Word Wisdom Dictionary to be sure of the meaning of the word *stamina*. Write the definition here.

_____

afflictions

Read the sentence that uses the word *afflictions* and some of the sentences around it.

Look for context clues to the word's meaning. What **Definitions, Descriptions, or Synonyms** can you find?

_____

Think about the context clues. What other information do you know?

_____

Predict a meaning for the word *affliction*.

_____

Check your Word Wisdom Dictionary to be sure of the meaning of the word *affliction*. Which of the meanings for the word *affliction* fits the context?

_____

🔑 Unlock the Meanings

Guide Words Guide words can help you locate a word in a dictionary more quickly. A pair of guide words appears at the top of every dictionary page. The first guide word shows the *first* dictionary entry on the page. The second guide word shows the *last* dictionary entry on that same page. The word you are looking for will appear in alphabetical order between the two guide words.

Guide Words

classify   **clerk**

The word *clear* would appear on the same page as these guide words because it comes between them in alphabetical order.

Locate Guide Words Look up the following words in a classroom dictionary or use a dictionary in your library. Write the pair of guide words that appears at the top of the dictionary page for each of these words.

1 fracture _____

2 invalid _____

3 vigor _____

4 exhale _____

5 posture _____

Find the Words Here are pairs of guide words that appear at the top of a dictionary page. Find the word from the Word List on page 43 that would appear between them on each dictionary page.

6 compete _____ compose

7 staircase _____ stamp

8 natural _____ near

9 photograph _____ pick

10 affect _____ after

Find the Meaning

1. Use context clues.
2. Look for a familiar root, prefix, or suffix.
3. If the context or a word part doesn't help, check the dictionary.

WORD LIST

fracture
physical
stamina
posture
affliction
vigor
invalid
nausea
exhale
complexion

Define the Words   Follow the steps above to write the meaning of each boldfaced word. Write 1, 2, or 3 to show which steps you used.

1 The symptoms of food poisoning may include **nausea** and cramps.

_____

2 Sonya's pale **complexion** forced her to use sunscreen all year long.

_____

3 Mom cared for Aunt Jen, who was temporarily an **invalid** after her surgery.

_____

4 One way to measure **physical** fitness is to see how far you can run.

_____

5 Palace guards maintain a straight **posture** and a serious facial expression.

_____

6 Some of the stories about early settlers describe disease, pain, and **affliction**.

_____

7 The doctor told José to **exhale** completely before filling his lungs with air.

_____

8 Jaime used crutches and wore a cast on his ankle until the **fracture** healed.

_____

9 The body needs vitamins and minerals to maintain its **vigor**.

_____

10 The mountain climber built her **stamina** by climbing flights of stairs.

_____

Process the Meanings

WORD LIST

fracture

physical

stamina

posture

affliction

vigor

invalid

nausea

exhale

complexion

Use Context Clues Write the word from the Word List that best completes each sentence. You may need to add an ending to a word. Underline the parts of the sentence that helped you make your decision.

1 Several of the _____ sat in their wheelchairs on the porch of the hospital.

2 Some people think weight gain in children is related to a reduction in _____ education programs in the schools.

3 If you suspect that a person may have a _____, support the injured part with a splint while waiting for emergency help.

4 If you quickly spin around many times, _____ may result.

5 There is no obvious reason why some people have skin problems while others have a smooth, clear _____.

6 "Good _____, people! Shoulders back! Chin up! Stomach tucked! Now glide!" the modeling coach instructed.

7 In an emergency rise to the surface, the scuba diver must remember to _____ to avoid lung damage that might result from holding her breath.

8 In a triathlon, athletes must have the _____ to bike, swim, and run long distances.

9 With great _____, Dillon chopped several logs into firewood.

10 Grandmother always said that being old is a state of mind, not an _____.

Apply What You've Learned

Use Words Correctly Answer **yes** or **no** to each question. Then explain your answer.

1 Can a metal flagpole exhibit **vigor**?

_____

2 Would you feel like eating a big meal if you suffered from **nausea**?

_____

3 Would someone with **stamina** be helpful if you had a lot of furniture to move?

_____

4 Does **posture** refer to the length of the strides a person takes while walking?

_____

5 Might a person wear a hat to protect his or her **complexion**?

_____

6 Would you expect a doctor to treat a **fracture** with cough medicine?

_____

7 Is an **affliction** a cause of pain and suffering?

_____

8 Could a highly **physical** dance program be filled with leaps and twirls?

_____

9 Would you expect to find an **invalid** working at a construction site?

_____

10 If you **exhale,** do you gulp air as quickly as possible?

_____

Write It! How are you feeling today? Write a poem that describes your energy level and your sensations. Use as many words as you can from the Word List on page 44.

Review

for Word Wisdom

Categorize the Words   Decide which of the following categories each word from the Word List belongs in. Write each word in the correct column. Then circle the words that have the root *sens*, *spir*, or *corp*. Two words come from these roots but are not spelled the same.

WORD LIST

physiology
respiration
sensitive
symptom
benign
potent
corps
constitution
rejuvenate
inflammation
sensory
sensation
corset
corporal
expire
aspirate
corpse
sensible
desensitize
perspire
fracture
physical
stamina
posture
affliction
vigor
invalid
nausea
exhale
complexion

Good Health	Neutral	Poor Health

Check the Meanings If the underlined word is used correctly, write **C**. If the underlined word is used incorrectly, write **I**.

_____ **1** An <u>invalid</u> trains for a marathon.

_____ **2** An <u>inflammation</u> may be red and swollen.

_____ **3** If you've lost <u>sensation</u> in your fingers, you will have a hard time playing the piano.

_____ **4** Someone with good <u>posture</u> tends to slump a little while sitting at the dinner table.

_____ **5** A <u>physiology</u> textbook would explain how the different organs of the body work.

_____ **6** Most people <u>perspire</u> on extremely cold, windy days.

_____ **7** Doctors check <u>respiration</u> by looking into their patients' ears.

_____ **8** Good care for a healthy <u>complexion</u> is daily washing with a mild soap and using sunscreen for protection from the sun.

_____ **9** A <u>sensory</u> experience would include sounds, tastes, smells, and textures, as well as sights.

_____ **10** A <u>symptom</u> of a disease is its complete cure.

Match the Antonyms Match the antonyms in the right column to the vocabulary words in the left column. Write the letter of your answer on the line.

Vocabulary Word	Antonym
11 benign _____	a. recover
12 potent _____	b. breathe in
13 expire _____	c. harmful
14 affliction _____	d. benefit
15 exhale _____	e. weak

TEST-TAKING STRATEGY

Feeling nervous before a test is normal. But it's easy to overcome.

• Make sure you're ready. Create a sample test and answer the questions. Give yourself the same amount of time to complete the test as you'll have in class.

• Don't start answering the questions until you look at the whole test. Figure out which parts will be easiest and which will be hardest. Decide how much time you'll need for each part.

• Keep a positive attitude. If you think you can do well, you will.

Sample:

Each of the answer choices below makes sense, but only one has the same meaning as the underlined word.

to perspire a little
- ○ laugh
- ○ breathe
- ● sweat
- ○ exercise

Practice Test   Fill in the circle of the answer that has the SAME or ALMOST THE SAME meaning as the underlined word.

1 a potent new medicine
- ○ experimental
- ○ powerful
- ○ weak
- ○ expensive

2 a bone with a fracture
- ○ growth
- ○ bend
- ○ break
- ○ bruise

3 an uncomfortable but necessary corset
- ○ body support
- ○ criticism
- ○ question
- ○ public display

4 the diplomatic corps
- ○ building
- ○ code
- ○ uniform
- ○ group

5 a cure for nausea
- ○ stomach sickness
- ○ broken heart
- ○ bad mood
- ○ sore thumb

6 to aspirate blood from the wound
- ○ search for
- ○ increase
- ○ remove
- ○ test

7 benign clouds in the sky
- ○ dark
- ○ harmless
- ○ shapely
- ○ accumulating

8 to exhale completely
- ○ breathe out
- ○ breathe in
- ○ give up
- ○ turn over

9 a sensible diet
- ○ tasty
- ○ high calorie
- ○ simple
- ○ intelligent

10 corporal punishment
- ○ painful
- ○ well-deserved
- ○ minor
- ○ bodily

Play with Language

1 SONTONCUTITI: This is a synonym for your body or a state document.

_____

2 PEXRIE: You might use this verb to tell about an animal that is about to die or about a library card that is about to come to an end.

_____

3 RECSOP: A murder mystery might revolve around this object.

_____

4 TESVINSEI: Most people are this to the odor of a skunk.

_____

5 FACTOFLINI: Anything from a broken ankle to a bad cold can be this.

_____

6 ZISDIETENSE: You might have to do this to minimize allergies to cat or dog hair.

_____

7 HAYSPLIC: This adjective describes bodily activity or a type of exam.

_____

8 RIVOG: This noun describes the physical or mental energy of people or the strength of plants.

_____

9 NURJAVEETE: A cold drink on a hot day may do this to you.

_____

10 ATNAMIS: The average person would need this to paint a large room in a single day.

_____

Speak It! Go back to the answers you wrote for items 1–10 on page 47. With a class partner, discuss the sentences you marked with an I. Decide how to make each sentence correct. Say the corrected sentences aloud.

PART 1

Context Clues
for Word Wisdom

An Original in Life and Art:
Isadora Duncan

Someone once said, "Behavior is what a person does, not what he or she thinks, feels, or believes." In the case of Isadora Duncan, though, action and belief worked together. Read about this famous dancer who turned feeling into movement and created an art form to express the human spirit.

Isadora Duncan was born in 1878 in San Francisco, California. From the beginning, she was a rebel. School was not her **forte**. Instead of the classroom, she preferred the freedom of dancing on the beach.

Duncan found ballet instruction much too stiff and predictable. She was also convinced that dancing on her toes went against nature. Unlike her more obedient classmates, she had the **audacity** to follow her own vision of dance.

At sixteen, Duncan began to teach dance to children. She instructed them to imitate movements of nature. She had them dance to a favorite poem. Above all, Duncan urged them to be **authentic** dancers, not imitators.

Working without a partner, scenery, or ballet slippers, Duncan relied on facial expression and body movement to create moods and tell stories. With straight shoulders and raised chin, she could lead a shadow army. She **exuded** energy, strength, and emotion.

Duncan's early career was not very successful. Audiences found her skipping and whirling **bizarre** rather than creative. For a long time, she was too **exotic** for Americans used to more familiar ballet steps and positions. Unlike people who give up easily, however, Duncan remained

tenacious. Gradually, she discovered people who were not shocked by her art. Performances for important supporters of dance led to European tours.

Although her American reception had been lukewarm, audiences abroad found her performances **captivating**. Inspired by her talent, the European art world created sculpture, jewelry, poetry, novels, photographs, and murals in her honor.

In 1904 in Germany, Duncan used her money to open her first school of dance. Selecting children from poor families, she provided for their care and education. Schools in Paris and Moscow followed. Duncan herself led classes. Despite the fact that she was not very tall, she was a **stately** presence in her flowing Greek tunic, bare feet, and trailing scarf.

Sadly, Duncan's love of rippling scarves and shawls led to her death in France in 1927. Climbing into a sports car, she did not notice that a loose end of her red shawl had fallen over the side. As the car set off, the shawl caught in the rear wheel and broke her neck.

Although Isadora Duncan left no schools or dance patterns, today she is hailed as the mother of modern dance. She is remembered as a **visionary** who gave the world a new concept of strength and beauty.

Personality

UNIT 3

Context Clues Strategy

Look for What the Word Is Contrasted With

EXAMPLE: Mark is *reticent* about his painting despite the fact that he talks freely about the rest of his life.

CLUE: The words *despite the fact that he talks freely* contrast the word *reticent* with something familiar. You can conclude that *reticent* means the opposite of talking freely.

Here is another strategy for using context clues to figure out the meanings of new words. Here are the steps for using this context clues strategy to figure out the meaning of *tenacious*, which appeared in the article on page 50.

Read the sentence with the unknown word and some of the sentences around it.

· · · · ·

Unlike people who give up easily, however, Duncan remained **tenacious***. Gradually, she discovered people who were not shocked by her art.*

Look for context clues. What clues showing **What the Word Is Contrasted With** can you find?

· · · · ·

Duncan was *unlike people who give up easily,* so *tenacious* must mean the opposite of "giving up easily."

Think about the context clues and other helpful information you already know.

· · · · ·

It sounds as if Duncan held on to her vision of dance even though others didn't understand it.

Predict a meaning for the word.

· · · · ·

Tenacious must mean "holding on to something."

Check your Word Wisdom Dictionary to see how it defines the word.

· · · · ·

The word *tenacious* means "holding firmly to something."

Practice the Strategy Here are two of the boldfaced words from the article on page 50. Use the context clues strategy on page 51 to figure out the meaning of each word.

captivating

Read the sentence that uses the word *captivating* and some of the sentences around it.

Look for context clues. What clues showing **What the Word Is Contrasted With** can you find?

_____

Think about the context clues. What other information do you know?

_____

Predict a meaning for the word *captivating*.

_____

Check your Word Wisdom Dictionary to be sure of the meaning of the word *captivating*. Write the definition here.

_____

_____

stately

Read the sentence that uses the word *stately* and some of the sentences around it.

Look for context clues. What clues showing **What the Word Is Contrasted With** can you find?

_____

Think about the context clues. What other helpful information do you know?

_____

Predict a meaning for the word *stately*.

_____

Check your Word Wisdom Dictionary to be sure of the meaning of the word *stately*. Write the definition here.

_____

_____

forte

audacity

authentic

exude

bizarre

exotic

✔ tenacious

✔ captivating

✔ stately

visionary

Use Context Clues   You have been introduced to three words from the article on page 50. These words have been checked off in the Word List. Write the other seven words from the Word List in the first column. Predict a meaning for each word in the second column. Then look up the meaning of the word in your Word Wisdom Dictionary. In the third column, write the dictionary meaning that fits the context.

Vocabulary Word	Your Prediction	Dictionary Says
1		
2		
3		
4		
5		
6		
7		

Process the Meanings

Identify Synonyms or Antonyms Choose the correct synonym or antonym for each boldfaced word. Write the synonym or antonym on the line.

WORD LIST

forte

audacity

authentic

exude

bizarre

exotic

tenacious

captivating

stately

visionary

1 **exotic** (antonym) _____

    a. natural   b. familiar   c. foreign   d. stylish

2 **stately** (synonym) _____

    a. lawfully   b. dull   c. clearly   d. impressive

3 **authentic** (antonym) _____

    a. reliable   b. helpless   c. fake   d. generous

4 **forte** (synonym) _____

    a. talent   b. loudness   c. stronghold   d. discussion

5 **audacity** (antonym) _____

    a. perfection   b. fear   c. rejection   d. worthlessness

6 **exude** (synonym) _____

    a. insert   b. descend   c. inhale   d. ooze

7 **captivating** (antonym) _____

    a. unnoticeable   b. specific   c. noisy   d. ugly

8 **tenacious** (synonym) _____

    a. easygoing   b. colorful   c. firm   d. fierce

9 **visionary** (antonym) _____

    a. reward   b. assistant   c. realist   d. dreamer

10 **bizarre** (synonym) _____

    a. typical   b. strange   c. crowded   d. elegant

Apply What You've Learned

Use the Words Correctly Complete each sentence by writing the phrase that best explains the boldfaced word.

1 Your **captivating** personality may _____

a. chase away others.   b. draw others like a magnet.

2 Someone with **audacity** is likely to _____

a. become a trapeze artist.   b. be easily frightened.

3 **Bizarre** events are part of _____

a. a description of a typical day.   b. a science fiction story.

4 If your memory is **tenacious**, you _____

a. remember things for a long time.   b. forget things easily.

5 If you are a **visionary**, you _____

a. never dream about new things.   b. take risks and hope for good timing.

6 If you had an **authentic** Roman coin, you would be _____

a. happy about its value.   b. disappointed that it wasn't real.

7 If your friend **exudes** cheerfulness, _____

a. you will enjoy the person's good spirits.   b. you will stay away from your friend.

8 Your **forte** refers to _____

a. your weaknesses.   b. your special skills or talents.

9 **Exotic** foods might include _____

a. hamburgers and hot dogs.   b. tempeh and bird's nest soup.

10 A photo of a **stately** swan would show its _____

a. majestic beauty.   b. unfriendly disposition.

Write It! Describe someone you know or someone you've read about who has vision. Use as many vocabulary words from Part 1 as you can.

PART 2 Latin Roots

for Word Wisdom

Winston Churchill:
Courageous and Determined

Winston Churchill is famous for leading Great Britain to victory during World War II. However, he was not always a leader.

Born in 1874, Winston Churchill had a British father and an American mother. His wealthy parents left his care to nannies. Early on, Churchill was a shy, average student. Then he entered Sandhurst, a military academy. Young Winston did well there and discovered a skill in military planning.

Churchill joined the military after graduating from Sandhurst at the top of his class. Not **contented** with just one role, he also worked as a journalist. As a reporter, he covered a war that England was fighting in South Africa. Churchill was captured by enemy troops but escaped. He returned to Great Britain and became a national hero.

This admiration did not make him **conceited,** but it did give him great confidence. No longer shy and **staid,** Churchill found a home in politics. Over the following years, he ran for several offices. Although he was **contentious,** Churchill had many successes. He also had a few failures. Still, his finest hour was yet to come—Adolf Hitler's **deceitful** tactics were gaining him power in Germany. Soon Churchill's **impertinent** manner would suit him well.

In 1940, Churchill became prime minister, or leader, of Great Britain. By then, Hitler had invaded parts of Europe and was poised to conquer England. But, Churchill was **incapable** of accepting defeat. He began a **steadfast** campaign to gain support from the United States. In August 1941, President Franklin Roosevelt was **receptive** to Churchill's pleas. Four months later, Japan attacked Pearl Harbor. Then the United States joined Great Britain in fighting Japan and Germany.

Great Britain and its allies won the war in 1945. Churchill played a major role, but he lost an election that same year. He was no longer prime minister. Churchill did not give up politics, however—he regained his position in 1951. In 1955, poor health forced him to resign. He spent the final years of his life writing. His work includes histories of World Wars I and II. He also wrote *A History of the English-Speaking Peoples*. In 1953, Churchill received the Nobel Prize for Literature.

Often **obstinate,** Churchill once said, "It is a fine thing to be honest, but it is also very important to be right." Churchill did what he knew to be right. In 1963, he was made an honorary citizen of the United States. When Churchill died in 1965, the entire world praised his leadership. Once shy, he rose to lead his nation to victory. His record still inspires others to be "right," no matter the cost.

Practice the Context Clues Strategy Here are two of the boldfaced words from the essay on page 56. Use the context clues strategy you learned in Part 1 on page 51 to figure out the meanings of these words.

conceited

Read the sentence that uses the word *conceited* and some of the sentences around it.

Look for context clues to the word's meaning. What clues showing **What the Word Is Contrasted With** can you find?

_____

Think about the context clues. What other information do you know?

_____

Predict a meaning for the word *conceited*.

_____

Check your Word Wisdom Dictionary to be sure of the meaning of the word *conceited*. Write the definition here.

_____

contentious

Read the sentence that uses the word *contentious* and some of the sentences around it.

Look for context clues to the word's meaning. What clues showing **What the Word Is Contrasted With** can you find?

_____

Think about the context clues. What other information do you know?

_____

Predict a meaning for the word *contentious*.

_____

Check your Word Wisdom Dictionary to be sure of the meaning of the word *contentious*. Write the definition here.

_____

Unlock the Meanings

Several words you studied in Part 1 have Latin roots. Knowing the meaning of these roots can help you unlock the meaning of many unfamiliar words.

Latin Root: **cap, cept, cei**
meaning: to take; to seize
English word: *captivating*
meaning: seizing the attention or affection of; intensely fascinating

Latin Root: **ten, tin**
meaning: to hold
English word: *tenacious*
meaning: holding firmly

Latin Root: **sta, stea, sti**
meaning: to stand
English word: *stately*
meaning: standing tall; impressive; grand

WORD LIST

- contented
- conceited
- staid
- contentious
- deceitful
- impertinent
- incapable
- steadfast
- receptive
- obstinate

Categorize by Roots Find these roots in the Word List. Write each word in the correct column. Think of other words you know that come from the same Latin roots.

Latin Root:
cap, cept, cei

Latin Root:
ten, tin

Latin Root:
sta, stea, sti

Personality

Prefix	Meaning
im-	not
ob-	against

Example

ob- (against) + **sti** (stand) + **-nate** (adj.) = **obstinate**

Use Roots and Prefixes Circle any root and any prefix you find in the boldfaced words below. Use context clues, roots, and prefixes to write the meaning of each word. Check your definitions in your Word Wisdom Dictionary.

1 **Deceitful** advertising can fool consumers who believe the claims in commercials.

_____

2 Dad gave a **contented** smile as he tilted his chair and prepared for a nap.

_____

3 All her life, Lucy was **steadfast** in her dream of being an astronaut.

_____

4 Grandmother is a modern woman and is **receptive** to new ideas.

_____

5 Dealing with **obstinate** people is frustrating, as nothing changes their minds.

_____

6 Carly is not **conceited**; she checks her hair because she hates her haircut.

_____

7 The surgeon was annoyed at the **impertinent** interruptions from the patient.

_____

8 Behind the **staid** exterior of the gray house bloomed a fantasy of color.

_____

9 Have you ever been in a **contentious** mood and argued about silly topics?

_____

10 Larry gave up singing because he feels he is **incapable** of carrying a tune.

_____

Process the Meanings

WORD LIST

- contented
- conceited
- staid
- contentious
- deceitful
- impertinent
- incapable
- steadfast
- receptive
- obstinate

Solve the Clues Choose the word from the list that solves each clue.

1 These people need very long arms so they can pat themselves on the back. _____

2 If you say that the sky is blue, this kind of person will disagree just to argue. _____

3 Long ago, calling an older person by his or her first name was considered this. _____

4 If your dog refuses to go into the house, he is being this. _____

5 You may feel this way sitting under a tree on a warm summer day. _____

6 If your parents agree with your reasons for a larger allowance, they can be described as this. _____

7 People who lie are this. _____

8 If people haven't learned how to do something, they are this. _____

9 This kind of person is the opposite of fun and lively. _____

10 Everyone needs this kind of friend, one who will always be loyal. _____

Complete the Sentences Complete each sentence with a word from the Word List.

11 My boss is always _____ to my ideas.

12 A newborn baby is _____ of walking.

13 I'm happy and _____ to sit and read.

14 The marathon runner was _____ and didn't give up.

15 People who think they are perfect are _____.

Apply What You've Learned

Demonstrate Word Knowledge Answer each of the following questions by writing **yes** or **no** on the blank line. Underline other words in the sentence that helped you answer the question. Be prepared to discuss the reasons for your choices.

1 Would a coach who is **receptive** to new techniques be against change?

_____

2 Would you expect a **staid** dinner guest to wear a chicken costume?

_____

3 Is it **impertinent** to ask a person how much money he or she makes?

_____

4 Would someone **steadfast** in the defense of animal rights hunt deer for sport? _____

5 Do **conceited** people always say negative things about themselves?

_____

6 Is it difficult to have faith in a **deceitful** person? _____

7 Would the **contentious** crew of a sailboat have a hard time working together? _____

8 Is an **obstinate** horse the best mount for a new rider? _____

9 Would you worry about an accountant or a bank teller who is **incapable** of doing math? _____

10 Is a **contented** person willing to keep things just as they are? _____

Speak It! Describe your own personality to a class partner. First, think about your likes, dislikes, moods, and disposition. Write down your ideas before speaking about them. Reveal only those parts of your personality that you are comfortable sharing. Use as many words from the Word List on page 60 as you can.

PART 3 Reference Skills

for Word Wisdom

The Fury: Who Was Hitler?

Adolf Hitler certainly earned himself a place in history. But what kind of man was behind that angry scowl?

Adolf Hitler was born in Austria in 1889. He began school as a good student, but his high school grades greatly disappointed his father. Alois Hitler wanted his son to be a government worker like he was. However, young Adolf wanted to be an artist.

Still, Hitler failed the entrance exam for art school twice. Unable to find work, he sometimes spent the night on local park benches. **Indignant** about being homeless, Hitler looked for others who were "lower" than himself. He began to have a **condescending** attitude toward non-Germans. He had not actually been born in Germany, but somehow he considered himself to be German.

When World War I began, Hitler joined the German army. It was not just an **impulsive** act, as fighting in a war suited his angry personality. However, Germany lost the war and was forced to give up much of its territory. Far from accepting the situation, Hitler became even more **sullen**. He joined the Nazis and soon became the leader of the young political party. Hitler formed a **notorious** group called the Storm Troopers. They fought anyone trying to stop the Nazis.

In 1923, Hitler made a **pretentious** but ineffective show of power. About 2,000 of his Storm Troopers tried—and failed—to overturn the Bavarian government. Hitler was sent to prison for five years for treason, but he served only nine months. By the time of his release, his anger had reached new heights.

Hitler blamed all of Germany's problems on the Jewish people and the Communists. He vowed to rid Germany of them. In the meantime, his Nazi party grew in size and strength. By January 1933, the Nazis were so powerful that Hitler was appointed Chancellor of Germany. Yet that title was not enough for this **immodest** man. He quickly named himself the Fuehrer, or leader. As a dictator, he controlled all of Germany. Still, he wanted more.

Hitler insisted that certain people were "inferior." He established extermination camps to rid Germany and the world of Jewish people, handicapped people, mentally ill people, and many others. Men, women, and **timid** young children were herded into these **despicable** camps. As many as 12 million people died there.

Nearby nations grew nervous as Hitler gained power, but by the time they took **defensive** action, it was too late. More nations fell under Nazi control. Fortunately, the German army was defeated at Stalingrad, Russia. As the war turned against him, Hitler killed himself on April 30, 1945. Germany surrendered seven days later.

Hitler's anger, or fury, had ruled him—and many others. But his anger was not enough to keep him in power. Instead, it contributed to his downfall.

Practice the Context Clues Strategy Here are two of the boldfaced words from the essay on page 62. Use the context clues strategy you learned in Part 1 on page 51 to figure out the meanings of these words.

sullen

📖 **Read** the sentence that uses the word *sullen* and some of the sentences around it.

🔍 **Look** for context clues to the word's meaning. What clues showing **What the Word Is Contrasted With** can you find?

_____

💡 **Think** about the context clues. What other information do you know?

_____

➡️ **Predict** a meaning for the word *sullen*.

_____

✔️ **Check** your Word Wisdom Dictionary to be sure of the meaning of the word *sullen*. Write the meaning here.

_____

pretentious

📖 **Read** the sentence that uses the word *pretentious* and some of the sentences around it.

🔍 **Look** for context clues to the word's meaning. What clues showing **What the Word Is Contrasted With** can you find?

_____

💡 **Think** about the context clues. What other information do you know?

_____

➡️ **Predict** a meaning for the word *pretentious*.

_____

✔️ **Check** your Word Wisdom Dictionary to be sure of the meaning of the word *pretentious*. Which of the meanings for the word *pretentious* fits the context?

_____

Base Words and Derived Words
A **derived word** is formed by adding an ending to a base word and changing its part of speech. For example, adding the suffix *-ly* to the base word *sullen* turns the adjective *sullen* into the adverb *sullenly*. Derived words are usually listed at the end of the dictionary entry for the base word.

Sometimes a derived word has its own separate entry. In some dictionaries, for example, the adjective *condescending* is listed separately from the base word, which is the verb *condescend*.

If you can't find the word you're looking for in the dictionary, remember to check the derived words at the end of the entry for the base word.

Find Derived Words   Look in your Word Wisdom Dictionary for derived words from these base words. These words are from the Word List on page 65. Write a derived word for each base word.

1 despicable   _____

2 indignant   _____

3 sullen   _____

4 defensive   _____

5 notorious   _____

6 condescend   _____

7 timid   _____

8 impulsive   _____

9 immodest   _____

10 pretentious   _____

Find the Meaning

1. Use context clues.
2. Look for a familiar root, prefix, or suffix.
3. If the context or a word part doesn't help, check the dictionary.

WORD LIST

indignant

condescending

impulsive

sullen

notorious

pretentious

immodest

timid

despicable

defensive

Define the Words   Follow the steps above to write the meaning of each boldfaced word. Write 1, 2, or 3 to show which steps you used.

1 They are **notorious** for forgetting what they promised to do.

_____

2 Mooshlet, our Russian Blue, is a **timid** cat who hides under furniture.

_____

3 The ad makes **immodest** claims that the product is the best in the world.

_____

4 I don't have to hear George yell; his **sullen** expression shows his bad mood.

_____

5 Calling the modest little beach cottage Summer Castle is **pretentious**.

_____

6 Instead of respecting new artists, the famous sculptor gave them **condescending** advice.

_____

7 Cruelty toward animals is **despicable**.

_____

8 The coat was an **impulsive** purchase; Leanne had not planned on buying it.

_____

9 Some people are **defensive** even when receiving helpful advice.

_____

10 The community was **indignant** when it was criticized for its parade.

_____

Process the Meanings

WORD LIST

indignant

condescending

impulsive

sullen

notorious

pretentious

immodest

timid

despicable

defensive

Choose the Correct Word Write the word from the Word List that best completes each sentence. Then underline the parts of each sentence that helped you make your choice.

1 Some questions can put people on the _____, making them feel as if they have to explain their actions.

2 Leaders who bring out the worst in people can be responsible for _____ behavior.

3 Even though he acts shy, my brother is not _____ about trying new things.

4 Grandfather told the story of Jean Laffite, a _____ pirate who helped the United States in the War of 1812.

5 Although she is our boss, she is never _____, so everyone in our group feels equal.

6 Addressing infant twins as "Sir" and "Madam" seems _____ to me.

7 A _____ gray sky and a cold wind made the November afternoon feel gloomy.

8 Please don't think I'm _____ if I tell you how well I did on my math test.

9 There's nothing _____ about a dogsled race; it takes months of planning and practice.

10 We were _____ because no one had warned us that the ice cream store was closing early.

Apply What You've Learned

Associate the Meanings   Write the word from the Word List on page 66 that best answers each question below.

1 Which word describes someone who feels that people always question his decisions? _____

2 Which word do you associate with someone who makes sudden, on-the-spot decisions? _____

3 Which word goes with a well-known criminal? _____

4 Which word goes with being wrongfully accused?

_____

5 Which word describes someone who gives very hesitant answers to questions? _____

6 Which word goes with *grumpy* and *sulky*? _____

7 Which word describes someone who treats people as if they are not as smart as he or she is? _____

8 Which word describes someone who buys flashy, expensive cars and jewelry? _____

9 Which word describes someone who talks about himself in a way that is too proud? _____

10 Which word describes acts of cruelty and hatred?

_____

Write It!   Write a story in which the two main characters have opposite personalities. Use as many words from the Word List on page 66 as you can.

Review

for Word Wisdom

Sort by Prefixes Sort the words in the Word List by the prefixes below. Write each word in the correct column. If a word doesn't have one of the prefixes, write it in the column titled "none of the prefixes shown." Then circle every word that has the root *cap, cept,* or *cei; ten* or *tin;* and *sta, stea,* or *sti.*

WORD LIST

- forte
- audacity
- authentic
- exude
- bizarre
- exotic
- tenacious
- captivating
- stately
- visionary
- contented
- conceited
- staid
- contentious
- deceitful
- impertinent
- incapable
- steadfast
- receptive
- obstinate
- indignant
- condescending
- impulsive
- sullen
- notorious
- pretentious
- immodest
- timid
- despicable
- defensive

con-
(together; with)

de-
(remove; reduce)

none of the prefixes shown

in- or im-
(on; in; for; not)

ob-
(against)

ex-
(without; from)

Review the Meanings Each statement contains a boldfaced vocabulary word. Decide whether each sentence is true or false, and write **true** or **false** on the line.

_____ **1** A **captivating** tale of adventure would be a book you would probably return to the library without finishing.

_____ **2** A **defensive** attitude might be expected in a person who has a guilty conscience.

_____ **3** Such **exotic** plants as orchids and birds of paradise are common in most indoor and outdoor gardens.

_____ **4** Old names for hairstyles, such as _poodle, beehive,_ and _flip,_ have a **staid** sound to them.

_____ **5** Someone would need **audacity** to think that he could survive a long fall.

_____ **6** Schools have been known to ban T-shirts with certain **contentious** messages.

_____ **7** Rooftop devices like weather vanes were once **impulsive** ways to predict the weather.

_____ **8** If someone expects you to be **steadfast,** he or she requires you to freeze in place and remain motionless.

_____ **9** A person with a **sullen** expression would not be an appropriate member of a welcoming committee.

_____ **10** An **authentic** costume from a classic movie could be worth a lot of money today.

Complete the Word Group Choose a word from the Word List that completes each group of words.

11 specialty, skill, strong point _____

12 difficult, stubborn, unmoving _____

13 boastful, pompous, showy _____

14 fulfilled, happy, satisfied _____

15 reserved, shy, hesitant _____

Taking Vocabulary Tests

TEST-TAKING STRATEGY

Misunderstanding directions is one of the biggest reasons for disappointing test results.

• Before you begin a test, reread the directions to make sure you understand them.

• If you are allowed to write on the test, underline or circle the important words in the directions. For example, do the directions ask you to choose **synonyms** or **antonyms**?

This test asks you to find **synonyms**. If you were looking for antonyms by mistake, you would incorrectly fill in the first circle.

Sample:

authentic Greek coin
○ fake
○ ancient
○ beautiful
● genuine

Practice Test Fill in the circle for the word that is a synonym for the boldfaced word.

1 a **pretentious** monument to bad taste
○ thrilling
○ vivid
○ showy
○ solid

2 a **bizarre** coincidence
○ weird
○ happy
○ distant
○ extreme

3 **receptive** to change
○ negative
○ sorry
○ donated
○ open

4 **immodest** claims of great success
○ ideal
○ awkward
○ intelligent
○ boastful

5 encouraged to be less **obstinate**
○ stubborn
○ shallow
○ noisy
○ curious

6 **condescending** tone of voice
○ hoarse
○ complimentary
○ superior
○ matching

7 **timid** about speaking in public
○ confident
○ hesitant
○ sick
○ bored

8 actions designed to be **deceitful**
○ misleading
○ vengeful
○ forgiving
○ disregarded

9 **despicable** attempts to harm
○ repeated
○ extreme
○ terrible
○ half-hearted

10 **impertinent** arrival without an invitation
○ confusing
○ well-timed
○ rude
○ welcome

Build New Words

Use Suffixes to Turn Adjectives Into Nouns

Adding some suffixes to an adjective changes the adjective into a noun. All of the following suffixes can mean "the condition of being something," "the quality of being something," or "the state of being something."

-ness   -cy   -ty   -ity

Use these suffixes to make nouns from the vocabulary words below. You may have to drop, change, or add letters. Check your Word Wisdom Dictionary if you are not sure. Then write a sentence using each new word.

Vocabulary Word (Adjective)	+ Suffix	= Noun	Sentence
impulsive	-ness		
tenacious	-ty		
receptive	-ness		
obstinate	-cy		
incapable	-ity		

 Speak It! Describe a person you know well. Support your statements about the person with vivid examples that illustrate your point. Use as many of the vocabulary words from this Personality unit as you can.

Context Clues

for Word Wisdom

Living Under Glass:
Biosphere 2

International experts in science, agriculture, and engineering wondered if technology could change or repair the environment. Read this essay to find out whether the miniature world they created answered their questions.

In September 1991 in Arizona, eight people were sealed inside the largest greenhouse ever built. Along with them were four goats, three pigs, chickens, and more than 3,000 other species of animals and plants. All the living things had been carefully selected. Everything had to be easy to care for and useful. Even tiny forms of life like **microbes** had to play a part in this sealed environment.

For the next two years, these people, animals, and plants made their home in a living laboratory. The laboratory was named Biosphere 2. It combined all the things found on Earth that support life. By studying this **biosphere,** scientists hoped to understand the **interaction** of living things.

Almost everything the inhabitants would need for two years was housed under the eighty-five-foot-high, three-acre glass dome. Only sunlight and electricity came from outside. Engineers had hoped to produce electricity from sunlight. They found, however, that **solar** power was too expensive. Instead, a huge **artificial** waterfall supplied **hydroelectric** power to run generators.

Biosphere 2 was divided into seven areas. Each area duplicated a particular kind of environmental community. These **ecosystems** included everything from a tropical rain forest to a twenty-five-foot-deep ocean. Researchers could control salt and fresh water in the swamp area to test the growth of mangroves, those trees with aboveground roots so thick the roots look like tree trunks. Scientists could change the **terrain** of the farm environment to learn how different ground features affect the growth of crops. They could experiment with the effect of lack of water on the grasses of the **savanna.**

There were some successes. Eighty-seven new coral colonies formed under the glass dome. This was remarkable because of the fast rate at which reefs are dying in the real world. Surprisingly, tilapia, a kind of fish, multiplied in the rice paddies. The fish fed the crew as well as purifying the water and fertilizing the soil.

Overall, though, the experiment did not meet its goals. The glass dome leaked. Crop yields were low, and oxygen was limited. Ants overran the greenhouse. After four years, scientists decided that the artificial biosphere was not **viable.** They found that even with all of its brilliance, technology could not imitate life.

Context Clues Strategy

Look for What Kind of Object, Concept, or Action the Word Is

EXAMPLE: Any size *structure*—from a giant glass greenhouse to a tiny wooden maze for mice—can help scientists gather new information.

CLUE: The words *a giant glass greenhouse* and *a tiny wooden maze for mice* tell what kind of thing a structure is. A structure is something that is built or constructed.

One way to understand the meaning of new words is to use the context in which the word appears. Here are the steps for using this context clues strategy to figure out the meaning of the word *solar*, which appears in the essay you just read.

Read the sentence with the unknown word and some of the sentences around it.

• • • • •

*Engineers had hoped to produce electricity from sunlight. They found, however, that **solar** power was too expensive.*

Look for context clues. What clues showing **What Kind of Object, Concept, or Action the Word Is** can you find?

• • • • •

The words *solar power* seem to refer back to the words *electricity from sunlight*.

Think about the context clues and other information you already know.

• • • • •

Water and the sun are natural sources of energy. They can produce electricity.

Predict a meaning for the word.

• • • • •

The word *solar* probably means "related to the sun."

Check your Word Wisdom Dictionary to see how it defines the word.

• • • • •

Solar means "related to the sun."

Unlock the Meanings

Practice the Strategy   Here are two of the boldfaced words from the essay on page 72. Use the context clues strategy on page 73 to figure out the meaning of each word.

hydroelectric

Read the sentence that uses the word *hydroelectric* and some of the sentences around it.

Look for context clues. What clues showing **What Kind of Object, Concept, or Action the Word Is** can you find?

_____

Think about the context clues. What other information do you know?

_____

Predict a meaning for the word *hydroelectric*.

_____

Check your Word Wisdom Dictionary to be sure of the meaning of the word *hydroelectric*. Write the definition here.

_____

terrain

Read the sentence that uses the word *terrain* and some of the sentences around it.

Look for context clues. What clues showing **What Kind of Object, Concept, or Action the Word Is** can you find?

_____

Think about the context clues. What other information do you know?

_____

Predict a meaning for the word *terrain*.

_____

Check your dictionary to be sure of the meaning of the word *terrain*. Write the definition here.

_____

Use Context Clues You have been introduced to three vocabulary words from the essay on page 72. Those words are checked off in the Word List. Under "Vocabulary Word," write the other seven words from the Word List. Predict a meaning for each word under "Your Prediction." Then check the meanings in the Word Wisdom Dictionary. Write the definitions under "Dictionary Says."

WORD LIST

microbes
biosphere
interaction
✔ solar
artificial
✔ hydroelectric
ecosystem
✔ terrain
savanna
viable

	Vocabulary Word	Your Prediction	Dictionary Says
1			
2			
3			
4			
5			
6			
7			

⚙️ Process the Meanings

Use the Words Correctly in Writing   Rewrite each sentence in your own words. Use the word in parentheses in your sentence. You will need to add an ending to some words.

WORD LIST

microbes
biosphere
interaction
solar
artificial
hydroelectric
ecosystem
terrain
savanna
viable

1 Gravity is one of four things working with one another that hold everything on the planet together. (interactions)

_____

2 In northern forests, the natural community is home to moose, bears, and wolves. (ecosystem)

_____

3 Extremely tiny life forms can survive even in extreme environments. (microbes)

_____

4 Energy produced by water power is limited because there are few fast-moving rivers left. (hydroelectric)

_____

5 The banana made of plastic looked so real that I tried to eat it. (artificial)

_____

6 Power that comes from the sun is not always reliable because some days are cloudy or rainy. (solar)

_____

7 Harry realized that he needed a workable plan for getting his homework done. (viable)

_____

8 Cattle ranching is a major occupation of people living on the grasslands of South America. (savanna)

_____

9 Bumps of granite and twisted roots created rough surface features of an area of land. (terrain)

_____

10 We are all connected; we all live together in the earth's environment that maintains life. (biosphere)

_____

Apply What You've Learned

Use the Words Correctly Answer each question by writing **Yes** or **No** on the blank line. Write a sentence to explain your answer.

1 Can you see **microbes** without a microscope?

_____

2 Could sandy **terrain** slow down your running if you weren't used to it?

_____

3 If your cat ignores your dog, do your pets have frequent **interactions**?

_____

4 Is **solar** power a source for heat and electricity?

_____

5 Would you expect to find a **biosphere** on sale at a nature store?

_____

6 Is putting tape on a broken glass vase a **viable** way to repair it?

_____

7 Could a **hydroelectric** plant be built in any neighborhood?

_____

8 Would a small pond in your neighbor's yard be considered an **ecosystem**?

_____

9 Is *savanna* a synonym for *desert*?

_____

10 Would you have to water an **artificial** plant?

_____

Write It! Draw a picture or cut out a magazine illustration for two words from the Part 1 Word List. Write the definition of each word. Then write your own sentence using each word correctly.

PART 2

Latin and Greek Roots

for Word Wisdom

An Ancient Mystery:
Stonehenge

Many people have wondered about Stonehenge for centuries. Why was this circle of stones built? How was it built so long ago—over 5,000 years—before construction equipment was available?

Built in England over a period of more than a thousand years, Stonehenge was constructed in three phases. The first phase was simply a large ditch, or henge. The second phase was a complex design of timber posts. But the third phase is what people imagine when they think of Stonehenge.

In the third phase, about eighty bluestones were used to form a double circle. Each stone weighed up to four tons. They were transported from mountains 240 miles away. **Hydraulics** was not available to help lift or move these huge stones. They must have been dragged on rollers and pulled on sledges. For part of the way, they might have traveled on barges or boats. Loading the stones on and off the barges must have been very difficult. It certainly was not a task for someone with weak muscles or for someone with a fear of water, or **hydrophobia**.

Giant sarsen stones were also used to form an outer circle. These stones weighed up to fifty tons each. Like the bluestones, the sarsen stones did not come from the **territory** around Stonehenge. These huge stones were transported from an area twenty miles away.

Researchers marvel at the effort needed to build Stonehenge. Ringed by burial mounds, Stonehenge at one point must have been used as a site to **inter** the dead. Instead of being buried in deep **subterranean** graves, however, the dead were placed in shallow graves. Then soil was mounded over them.

One astronomer believes that Stonehenge was built as an early warning system for meteor storms. Pieces of a giant comet threatened to strike Earth about 5,000 to 5,500 years ago. These pieces were capable of exploding with the force of a **hydrogen** bomb. On the day of highest danger, the comet trail would have been aligned with the stones at Stonehenge. Perhaps some of the ditches were dug as shelters from falling meteors.

A few people think Stonehenge was not built by **terrestrial** people, but by outer space aliens. Though there is little evidence to support this, we do have evidence that an ancient people called the Beaker Folk helped build this monument. They placed the stones so they aligned with the sun during the summer and winter **solstices**. Perhaps they used Stonehenge as an open-air **solarium**.

Today, a highway, parking lots, gift shops, and inns are not far from Stonehenge. People can sit on inn **terraces** and view this amazing monument. The English Heritage group is trying to protect Stonehenge from its own popularity. The group wants to preserve Stonehenge for generations to come.

Practice the Context Clues Strategy   Here are two of the boldfaced words from the essay on page 78. Use the context clues strategy you learned in Part 1 on page 73 to figure out the meanings of these words.

territory

Read the sentence that uses the word *territory* and some of the sentences around it.

Look for context clues to the word's meaning. What clues showing **What Kind of Object, Concept, or Action the Word Is** can you find?

_____

Think about the context clues. What other helpful information do you know?

_____

Predict a meaning for the word *territory*.

_____

Check your Word Wisdom Dictionary to be sure of the meaning of the word *territory*. Which of the meanings for the word *territory* fits the context?

_____

subterranean

Read the sentence that uses the word *subterranean* and some of the sentences around it.

Look for context clues to the word's meaning. What clues showing **What Kind of Object, Concept, or Action the Word Is** can you find?

_____

Think about the context clues. What other helpful information do you know?

_____

Predict a meaning for the word *subterranean*.

_____

Check your Word Wisdom Dictionary to be sure of the meaning of the word *subterranean*. Write the definition here.

_____

Unlock the Meanings

Some of the words you studied in Part 1 have Latin and Greek roots. Knowing the meaning of these roots can help you unlock the meaning of many unfamiliar words. The roots below refer to the earth, the sky, and water.

Latin Root: **terr**

meaning: the earth

English word: *terrain*

meaning: land and its features; ground

Latin Root: **sol**

meaning: the sun

English word: *solar*

meaning: produced by or coming from the sun

Greek Root: **hydro**

meaning: water

English word: *hydroelectric*

meaning: using water power to produce electricity

WORD LIST

hydraulics

hydrophobia

territory

inter

subterranean

hydrogen

terrestrial

solstice

solarium

terrace

Categorize by Roots Find these roots in the Word List. Write each word in the correct column. Remember that spellings of roots can change. Think of other words you know that come from the same Latin and Greek roots. Write each word in the correct column.

Earth, Sky, and Water

Latin Root:
terr

Latin Root:
sol

Greek Root:
hydro

_____

_____

_____

_____

_____

_____

_____

_____

_____

_____

_____

_____

_____

_____

_____

_____

_____

_____

Prefix	Meaning	Example
sub-	under	**sub-** (under) + **terr** (earth) + **anean** (adj.) = **subterranean**

Use Roots and Prefixes   Circle the root and any prefix you find in the boldfaced words. Use roots, prefixes, and context clues to write the meaning of the word. Check your definitions in the Word Wisdom Dictionary.

1 A character in an Edgar Allan Poe short story takes revenge on an enemy and **inters** him alive in a tomb.

_____

2 Someone who suffers from **hydrophobia** would not want to swim or dive.

_____

3 The garden party was held on the **terrace** of the house.

_____

4 Although bears can swim, they are still considered **terrestrial** animals.

_____

5 Engineers study **hydraulics** to design machines that use the flow of liquids.

_____

6 The **solarium**, with its flowering plants, was a wonderful room in which to spend a sunny morning in the middle of winter.

_____

7 During the winter **solstice** the sun is at its southernmost position.

_____

_____

8 **Hydrogen** combines with oxygen to make water.

_____

9 Cats mark their **territory** with the scent glands in their foreheads and lips.

_____

10 Atlanta and Seattle have the remains of **subterranean** cities.

_____

WORD LIST

hydraulics
hydrophobia
territory
inter
subterranean
hydrogen
terrestrial
solstice
solarium
terrace

Choose the Correct Word Choose the vocabulary word that best applies to each clue.

1 _____ Early people made up myths about this position of the sun because they could not explain it scientifically.

2 _____ A forklift truck operates by this when it uses liquid pressure to raise and lower heavy objects.

3 _____ This could belong to a country, a salesperson, a rival team, or an animal.

4 _____ This is a colorless and odorless gas and is one of the ingredients in water.

5 _____ In these places below the ground, subways carry passengers.

6 _____ If people have this fear, they would refuse to travel by boat.

7 _____ A light, sunny room with lots of glass is called this.

8 _____ Most trees are not aquatic. They are this.

9 _____ In order to do this to a body, cemeteries must follow state and local rules.

10 _____ If you have a platform extending out from a house, you have this.

Find Examples Write **E** next to each sentence that is an example of the boldfaced vocabulary word being used correctly.

11 _____ At the **solarium**, we saw a movie about space.

12 _____ An empire expanded its **territory** by ruling more countries.

13 _____ He doesn't ride on roller coasters because he has **hydrophobia**.

14 _____ While exploring underground caves, scientists found a **subterranean** river.

15 _____ For my science project, I made a model of a **hydrogen** molecule.

Apply What You've Learned

Complete the Analogies Select the vocabulary word that best completes each analogy. The symbol **:** stands for "is to." The symbol **::** stands for "as."

1 Dark : darkroom :: light : _____.

2 Marry : wedding :: _____ : funeral.

3 Fish : aquatic :: dog : _____.

4 Balcony : apartment :: _____ : house.

Demonstrate Word Knowledge Identify the following statements as true or false by writing **true** or **false** on the blank line.

_____ **5** You can purchase a jar of **hydrogen** at the drugstore.

_____ **6** The brakes on a car follow the principles of **hydraulics** when they increase pressure on the brake fluid to slow the car down.

_____ **7** Summer begins officially on June 21 because it is the **solstice**, the day with the most hours of sunlight.

_____ **8** Climbing a mountain would be impossible for someone with **hydrophobia**.

_____ **9** Carlsbad Caverns and similar caves are **subterranean** rock and crystal formations far below the earth's surface.

_____ **10** An intruder who enters the **territory** of a nesting mother bird can expect trouble.

_____ **11** A **terrestrial** animal lives mostly in water.

_____ **12** If you **inter** something, you cover it up.

_____ **13** A **solarium** lets in lots of sunlight.

_____ **14** Someone with **hydrophobia** fears snakes.

_____ **15** A **terrace** is underground.

Speak It! Give an oral report about any vocabulary word in the Word List in Part 2. Use several other words from the list.

PART 3

Reference Skills

for Word Wisdom

An Endangered Resource:
Fuel From Fossils

Many people are concerned about our dependence on fossil fuels for energy. They worry that we will use up our supply. To prepare for our future, we should learn as much as possible about fossil fuels.

Fossil fuels, including coal, oil, and natural gas, were produced millions of years ago. For example, coal formed from the remains of plants that grew on land. These plants died naturally or were destroyed by fire or by severe weather, such as hurricanes, tornadoes, and **cyclones**. As these dead plants lay on the ground, they became buried under layers of soil. For centuries, the remains were pressed together by the tons of soil and rock above them. In time, the decaying material turned into coal.

Have you ever heard of **petrified** wood? You might wonder why some wood turns to coal, while some wood becomes rock. Wood becomes petrified in very dry climates. As water and wind carry away the decaying parts of the wood, minerals fill in the empty spaces. In time, the entire piece of wood turns to rock. However, petrified wood is not a fossil fuel and cannot be burned.

Oil is another fossil fuel. It formed from the remains of plants and animals that lived in the ocean. After they died, the remains **gravitated** toward the ocean floor. There, the **molecules** of matter slipped into the **crevasses** of rocks where they decayed. Over hundreds of years, this material **liquefied,** turning into pools of oil. Many oil deposits are now in desert areas, such as the Middle East. Other deposits are undersea. Large drilling platforms float above buried pools of this oil, sometimes many **nautical** miles from shore. The platforms insert pipes into the ocean floor and pump the oil up to the surface. Some of this oil is turned into **petroleum** and gasoline.

Like oil, natural gas is formed from organisms that died in the ocean. Gas is often found floating on top of oil pools. The fastest growing source of energy, natural gas burns with less pollution than oil or coal. It is often used for heating and cooking.

Fossil fuels take centuries to form, and we use them much faster than they form. The world's nations often have **summit** meetings to discuss ways to conserve fossil fuels and use them fairly. Everyone wants to know how long our supplies will last, but that is a difficult question. It's like asking how long **cosmic** rays will shine from the sun. Many factors influence the answer. For example, new technology allows us to use energy more efficiently. New fuel deposits are sometimes discovered. Political, social, and economic factors also affect the production and use of energy. Still, we must work together with other nations to protect our limited supply of these fuels.

Practice the Context Clues Strategy Here are two of the boldfaced words from the essay on page 84. Use the context clues strategy you learned in Part 1 on page 73 to figure out the meanings of these words.

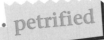
petrified

📖 **Read** the sentence that uses the word *petrified* and some of the sentences around it.

🔍 **Look** for context clues to the word's meaning. What clues showing **What Kind of Object, Concept, or Action the Word Is** can you find?

_____

💡 **Think** about the context clues. What other helpful information do you know?

_____

➡️ **Predict** a meaning for the word *petrified*.

_____

✔️ **Check** your Word Wisdom Dictionary to be sure of the meaning of the word *petrified*. Which of the meanings for the word *petrified* fits the context?

_____

liquefy

📖 **Read** the sentence that uses the word *liquefy* and some of the sentences around it.

🔍 **Look** for context clues to the word's meaning. What clues showing **What Kind of Object, Concept, or Action the Word Is** can you find?

_____

💡 **Think** about the context clues. What other helpful information do you know?

_____

➡️ **Predict** a meaning for the word *liquefy*.

_____

✔️ **Check** your Word Wisdom Dictionary to be sure of the meaning of the word *liquefy*. Write the definition here.

_____

🔑 Unlock the Meanings

Multiple Meanings   Some words have more than one meaning. When they do, each meaning may be listed separately with a superscript (raised) number. Dictionaries also use labels to help explain differences in meaning. Part-of-speech labels are usually abbreviated: *n.* for *noun*, *v.* for *verb*, and *adj.* for *adjective*.

When you look up a word in a dictionary, try to find the definition that best fits the context in which the word is used. Here are two dictionary entries that give different meanings for the vocabulary word *summit*.

sum•mit¹ /səm′ ət/ *n.* the highest point; the top. *We reached the summit of Mount Snow by noon.*
sum•mit² /səm′ ət/ *n.* meeting of high-level leaders. *The presidents of several countries met for a summit on economic policy.*

Choose the Correct Definition   Using the dictionary entries above, choose the correct definition for the word *summit* in each sentence below. Write the number of the definition (**1** or **2**) on the blank line.

1 Have you ever climbed to the summit of this hill? _____

2 If you could choose the summit of your life's work, what would it be? _____

3 Attending a summit on human rights is an important part of the prime minister's year. _____

4 The climbers celebrated when they reached the summit of Mount Mansfield. _____

5 The two countries decided to meet for a summit on achieving peace in the region. _____

Find the Meaning

1. Use context clues.
2. Look for a familiar root, prefix, or suffix.
3. If the context or a word part doesn't help, check the dictionary.

WORD LIST

cyclone
petrified
gravitate
molecule
crevasse
liquefy
nautical
petroleum
summit
cosmic

Define the Words Follow the steps above to write the meaning of each boldfaced word. Then write 1, 2, or 3 to show which steps you used.

1 A ship has to go about 6,076 feet to cover a **nautical** mile, which is almost 800 feet longer than a land mile.

_____

2 In May 1953, Sir Edmund Hillary and Tenzing Norgay became the first climbers to reach the **summit** of Mount Everest.

_____

3 Scientists believe that **cosmic** rays come from giant explosions of supernovas.

_____

4 The planets of our solar system **gravitate** toward the sun.

_____

5 If melted chocolate hardens, **liquefy** it in a double boiler over low heat.

_____

6 As Muir Glacier slowly melts, the **crevasse** on its surface continues to widen.

_____

7 Aunt Becky keeps a piece of **petrified** wood on her work table; it doubles as a paperweight and a hammer.

_____

8 In the Northern Hemisphere, the winds of a **cyclone** turn counterclockwise.

_____

9 Gasoline comes from the raw material **petroleum**, which is found underground.

_____

10 One atom of oxygen and two atoms of hydrogen form one **molecule** of water.

_____

Process the Meanings

WORD LIST

cyclone

petrified

gravitate

molecule

crevasse

liquefy

nautical

petroleum

summit

cosmic

Choose the Correct Word   Write the word from the Word List that best completes each sentence. You may have to add or change some word endings.

1 Signal flags, compasses, and sea charts contributed to the

_____ theme of the party.

2 The tourist looked out the window of the helicopter, peering into the blue

depths of the _____.

3 Hurricanes, typhoons, and _____ differ in the

forcefulness and pattern of the winds.

4 Have you ever noticed that people at a party _____

toward the kitchen?

5 One of our most fascinating national parks protects

_____ trees, which were turned to stone by the

action of minerals in water.

6 In a solid, the _____ are held together tightly.

7 It wasn't until I took an astronomy class that I became aware of the

_____ wonders of the world.

8 Because of their fear of heights, Erica and Hal stopped halfway up the cliff

and never saw the view from the _____.

9 Thick, highly flammable _____ is found beneath

the earth's surface.

10 To fuse the two pieces of glass, Alan _____ them in

a high-temperature kiln and then cooled them slowly.

Use the Words Correctly   Decide on the answer to each question. Base your answer on the meaning of the boldfaced word. Write **yes** or **no** on the blank line.

1 Would you expect a new book about **cosmic** theories to have down-to-earth suggestions about national parks? _____

2 Could you use a microwave oven to **liquefy** frozen soup? _____

3 Would people be likely to see a natural **crevasse** inside an art museum? _____

4 Would it be safe to go sailing during a **cyclone**? _____

5 Would you have to be careful of falling into a **summit**? _____

6 Do two friends **gravitate** toward each other? _____

7 Would **nautical** references refer to World War II land and air battles? _____

8 Is **petroleum** an important natural resource? _____

9 Is the fossil of an ancient **petrified** worm or insect alive? _____

10 Do hydrogen and oxygen **molecules** combine to form water? _____

Write It!   Choose three words from the Word List in Part 3 and use them as the basis of product names. Then write advertising that will make people eager to buy the product. Use as many other words from Part 3 as you can.

PART 4

Review

for Word Wisdom

Sort by Parts of Speech Sort the Word List by the part-of-speech categories below. Write each word in the correct column. Circle every word that has the root *hydro, terr,* or *sol*. Cross off each word in the list as you work.

WORD LIST

- microbes
- biosphere
- interaction
- solar
- artificial
- hydroelectric
- ecosystem
- terrain
- savanna
- viable
- hydraulics
- hydrophobia
- territory
- inter
- subterranean
- hydrogen
- terrestrial
- solstice
- solarium
- terrace
- cyclone
- petrified
- gravitate
- molecule
- crevasse
- liquefy
- nautical
- petroleum
- summit
- cosmic

Nouns	Verbs	Adjectives

Review the Meanings   Write the word from the Word List that best completes each sentence. You may have to add or change an ending.

1 After its first idea failed, the group brainstormed to find other

_____ solutions.

2 Cleaning a wound with soap and water will remove many of the

_____ that might cause infection.

3 During the summer _____ we watched the sun rise on

the longest day of the year.

4 If only dirty socks would _____ on their own toward

the washing machine, we wouldn't have to look for them.

5 There's a certain art to melting butter; it has to _____

but not separate or burn.

6 The salt marsh _____ is the home of many

endangered species.

7 A _____ in a house in Arizona might become too

warm and too expensive to air-condition.

8 That wood became _____ because water and minerals

seeped into its decaying cells and turned to stone.

9 The cement _____ off the dining room was an exotic

place with climbing vines and pots of orchids.

10 Was it a _____ or a tornado that swept Dorothy and

Toto all the way from Kansas to Oz?

Review

Taking Vocabulary Tests

TEST-TAKING STRATEGY

Some vocabulary tests have you decide which of several words best completes a sentence. Often, two answer choices may be related to the topic. Yet only one will actually complete the sentence. A wrong answer may be the wrong part of speech, or it may have the wrong meaning. Read all of the answer choices before you pick one answer. Check your answer by saying the sentence to yourself and replacing the blank with your answer. Make sure that the sentence makes sense.

Sample:
The climber fell into a
_____.

- ○ savanna
- ● crevasse
- ○ summit

Practice Test Fill in the circle for the word that best completes each sentence.

1 We climbed for days to reach the mountain's _____.
- ○ terrace
- ○ summit
- ○ territory

2 My class will _____ the time capsule in the ground.
- ○ inter
- ○ gravitate
- ○ liquefy

3 The salesperson covered her _____ in two weeks.
- ○ ecosystem
- ○ savanna
- ○ territory

4 Horses are _____ animals.
- ○ solar
- ○ terrestrial
- ○ subterranean

5 The _____ cavern was dark.
- ○ solar
- ○ hydroelectric
- ○ subterranean

6 Oil is made of _____.
- ○ petroleum
- ○ biosphere
- ○ territory

7 The uneven _____ made it hard to walk.
- ○ molecule
- ○ terrain
- ○ interaction

8 _____ is a type of gas.
- ○ Savanna
- ○ Cyclone
- ○ Hydrogen

9 The blue waves painted on the walls gave the room a _____ look.
- ○ nautical
- ○ viable
- ○ petrified

10 The crowd _____ toward the stage to hear the band.
- ○ inters
- ○ liquefies
- ○ gravitates

Play with Language

Solve a Crossword Puzzle Use the clues to fill in the crossword puzzle.

Across

1 Relating to the universe

3 In CO_2, one of these is carbon and two are oxygen.

6 Water power

7 Manufactured

8 Science dealing with liquids

10 Grassland

Down

2 Things acting on each other

4 Fear of water

5 Energy from the sun

9 Deep crack in a glacier's surface

Speak It! You've been hired to create the settings for a science-fiction movie that takes place in 2030. Describe some settings that are background for the action. Use as many words from this unit as you can.

Context Clues

for Word Wisdom

A Land Divided but a World United:
The Panama Canal

The Panama Canal was an incredible achievement in engineering. Since the beginning of the twentieth century, this artificial waterway has aided movement between the Atlantic and Pacific Oceans.

The country of Panama is a narrow strip of land in Central America, with the Atlantic Ocean on one side and the Pacific Ocean on the other. For hundreds of years, people had been interested in that strip of land. If a canal could be cut through it, ships would not have to travel all the way around the tip of South America in order to head north to get to parts of North America. Furthermore, many dangers could be **surmounted** if a link existed between the two oceans.

Several United States presidents **initiated** studies by sending engineers to Panama. However, all the studies ended with the same decision. The terrain would make it too difficult to build a canal. Swamps, mountains, jungles, and flooded rivers would **impede** progress, blocking workers and machines.

Ferdinand de Lesseps of France, who built the Suez Canal in Egypt, thought he could accomplish the same task in Panama. By 1888, however, poor planning and lack of funds had **paralyzed** the project. The French company sold its equipment to the United States, and in 1903 Panama and the United States signed a treaty. The agreement gave the United States permission to build a canal and to control an area called the Panama Canal Zone.

The project did not **proceed** smoothly. As time went by, illness, accidents, and high worker turnover had a **gradual** negative effect. The task was much more difficult than anyone had guessed. Taking a step back from the actual work, engineers spent the next four years preparing. They bought equipment, **marshaled** a labor force, and built housing for many workers. When the digging **resumed** in 1907, they were ready. Workers with dynamite and steam shovels cut their way across the land.

The Panama Canal was completed in seven years—ahead of schedule and under budget. It included artificial lakes and a **flexible** system of locks and dams. The lakes are eight feet above sea level on each side of a mountain range. Using hydraulics, the locks raise and lower ships to and from the lakes.

The canal turned a 7,000-mile trip around South America into a 51-mile trip. It shortened the sea voyage between New York and San Francisco from more than 15,000 miles to less than 6,100 miles. The Panama Canal opened to traffic on August 15, 1914. On December 31, 1999, the United States **relinquished** to Panama all rights to one of the most highly traveled waterways in the world.

Context Clues Strategy

Look for How Something Is Done

EXAMPLE: Workers *dredged* through swamps, jungles, and hills, bringing up dirt and rocks as they dug the waterway.

CLUE: The words *bringing up dirt and rocks* tell how dredging was done. The words *as they dug the waterway* also tell when and why dredging was done.

Here are the steps for using this context clues strategy to figure out the meaning of the word *surmounted*, which appears in the essay you just read.

Read the sentence with the unknown word and some of the sentences around it.

• • • • •

If a canal could be cut through it, ships would not have to travel all the way around the tip of South America in order to head north to get to parts of North America. Furthermore, many dangers could be **surmounted** *if a link existed between the two oceans.*

Look for context clues. What clues about **How Something Is Done** can you find?

• • • • •

The words *If a canal could be cut through it* tell the way that many dangers could be surmounted.

Think about the context clues and other helpful information you already know.

• • • • •

I know that people making sea voyages have to overcome dangers.

Predict a meaning for the word.

• • • • •

Surmount must mean "to overcome."

Check the Word Wisdom Dictionary to see how it defines the word.

• • • • •

The word *surmount* means "to conquer" or "to overcome."

Practice the Strategy Here are two of the boldfaced words from the essay on page 94. Use the context clues strategy on page 95 to figure out the meaning of these words.

Read the sentence that uses the word *impede* and some of the sentences around it.

Look for context clues. What clues about **How Something Is Done** can you find?

_____

Think about the context clues. What other helpful information do you know?

_____

Predict a meaning for the word *impede*.

_____

Check the Word Wisdom Dictionary to be sure of the meaning of the word *impede*. Write the definition here.

_____

paralyzed

Read the sentence that uses the word *paralyzed* and some of the sentences around it.

Look for context clues. What clues about **How Something Is Done** can you find?

_____

Think about the context clues. What other helpful information do you know?

_____

Predict a meaning for the word *paralyzed*.

_____

Check your dictionary to be sure of the meaning of the word *paralyzed*. Write the definition here.

_____

✔ surmount
initiate
✔ impede
✔ paralyze
proceed
gradual
marshal
resume
flexible
relinquish

Use Context Clues The three words you have learned from the essay on page 94 have a check mark next to them in the Word List. In the first column, write the other seven words from the Word List. In the second column, predict a meaning for each word using context clues. Check the Word Wisdom Dictionary. In the third column, write the dictionary meaning that fits the context.

Vocabulary Word	Your Prediction	Dictionary Says
1		
2		
3		
4		
5		
6		
7		

Process the Meanings

WORD LIST

- surmount
- initiate
- impede
- paralyze
- proceed
- gradual
- marshal
- resume
- flexible
- relinquish

Choose the Correct Word Write the word from the Word List that best completes each sentence. Use each word only once. You will need to add an ending to some words.

1 With a _____ schedule, Mom can set her own work hours.

2 The leader had to _____ the volunteers before starting the cleanup project.

3 The deer was _____ by fear and stood frozen in the open field.

4 People who have _____ problems can encourage others.

5 My dog wouldn't _____ my shoe, no matter how much I tugged and pleaded.

6 Terrence _____ a new fashion trend by wearing a keychain necklace.

7 Potholes in the road _____ traffic and made drivers miserable.

8 The plant's growth was _____, with one leaf appearing every few months.

9 Jodi's favorite show will _____ tonight after two weeks off the air.

10 Despite the rain, the balloon ride will _____ as scheduled.

Apply What You've Learned

Demonstrate Word Knowledge Answer the questions or follow the directions.

1 If you **proceed** with your latest project or interest, what will you do?

_____

2 Give an example of one way in which you can be more **flexible**.

_____

3 What new rule or policy would you like your school to **initiate**?

_____

4 How do you **surmount** problems when studying for a test?

_____

5 Describe a time when something **impeded** your way or progress.

_____

Use the Words Correctly Replace the underlined word or words with the correct word from the Word List. You will have to add an ending to some words.

6 Joe <u>gave up</u> his bus seat to a woman carrying a large suitcase.

_____

7 At the sudden noise, conversation stopped, but soon people <u>started</u> talking

again. _____

8 Gwen <u>organized</u> her friends for the volunteer group. _____

9 The strict rules <u>brought</u> the company's growth <u>to a stop</u>.

_____

10 The <u>gentle, step-by-step</u> rise of the trail made the hike easy.

_____

Write It! Research a major building project, such as the Golden Gate Bridge or the Hoover Dam. Write a brief report about how the work was done and what the challenges were. Use as many words from the Word List in Part 1 as you can.

PART 2

Latin Roots

for Word Wisdom

Moving Forward:
The Future of Our Schools

An editorial is a magazine or newspaper article that expresses an opinion about a specific topic. Some readers send in letters to the editor. Newspaper editors write editorials, like this one from the *Bedford Bugle*.

Election day is nearing. Bedford residents will decide whether we should build a new middle school. This decision will have long-lasting effects on our community. Should we spend more than three million dollars to build a new school, or should Bedford save its limited funds for an emergency? This newspaper strongly supports building a school that will meet the needs of our expanding population.

Bedford is proud to be one of the fastest-growing communities in the state. Almost as soon as a for-sale sign appears in a front yard, the home is sold. Two new developments are being completed north of town. As families flock to Bedford, the number of students in our schools increases. In 2000, only 142 students **graduated** from Bedford High School. Next year, that number will jump to 276. Our schools still **exceed** state standards in every form of measurement. Their excellence **reflects** our commitment to our children. However, we cannot expect students and teachers to continue to **succeed** as class sizes increase. For example, in the past three years, the average number of students in a kindergarten class has risen from eighteen to twenty-five students.

Yet when residents are asked to approve a tax increase to fund a new school building, many react by **reflex**. "We can't afford another school," they growl. Still, the value of our homes depends on the quality of our schools. The truth is, we cannot afford to crowd our children into our current schools. The quality of their education will suffer. In fact, our ranking in the state has already dropped by two points. If this continues, our schools may **regress** to where they were twenty years ago. Back then many families sent their children to private schools. We do not want to return to those days. A significant drop in the quality of our schools would also **precede** a decline in property values. Families will not want to move here.

Some people have tried to **deflect** attention from the need for a new school by pointing out the need for street repairs. Our streets should be repaved, but let's not **digress** from our main concern. If our children are going to **progress** and reach their potential, they need small classes and skilled teachers. We don't want to offer them a poor education.

Do we want smooth streets or educated children? In today's economy we can't have both. Which is more important to the people of Bedford? Vote for the tax levy. Show our children how much we value them.

Practice the Context Clues Strategy Here are two of the boldfaced words from the editorial on page 100. Use the context clues strategy you learned in Part 1 on page 95 to figure out the meanings of these words.

exceed

📖 **Read** the sentence that uses the word *exceed* and some of the sentences around it.

🔍 **Look** for context clues to the word's meaning. What clues about **How Something Is Done** can you find?

_____

💡 **Think** about the context clues and other information you know.

_____

➡️ **Predict** a meaning for the word *exceed*.

_____

✔️ **Check** your Word Wisdom Dictionary to be sure of the meaning of the word *exceed*. Write the definition here.

_____

regress

📖 **Read** the sentence that uses the word *regress* and some of the sentences around it.

🔍 **Look** for context clues to the word's meaning. What clues about **How Something Is Done** can you find?

_____

💡 **Think** about the context clues and other information you know.

_____

➡️ **Predict** a meaning for the word *regress*.

_____

✔️ **Check** your Word Wisdom Dictionary to be sure of the meaning of the word *regress*. Write the definition here.

_____

Unlock the Meanings

Several words you studied in Part 1 have Latin roots. Knowing the meaning of these roots can help you unlock the meaning of many unfamiliar words. Each root is related to movement.

Latin Root: **ced**
meaning: to go
English word: *proceed*
meaning: to go on or forward

Latin Root: **flec, flex**
meaning: to bend
English word: *flexible*
meaning: bendable, adaptable

Latin Root: **grad, gress**
meaning: to walk, to step
English word: *gradual*
meaning: by degrees; step by step

WORD LIST

graduate

exceed

reflect

succeed

reflex

regress

precede

deflect

digress

progress

Categorize by Roots Find these roots in the Word List. Write each word in the correct column. Then think of other words you know that come from the same Latin roots. Write each word in the correct column.

Latin Root: ced

Latin Root: flec, flex

Latin Root: grad, gress

_____

_____

_____

_____

_____

_____

_____

_____

_____

_____

_____

_____

_____

_____

_____

Movement

Prefix	Meaning
pre-	before
re-	back; again
di-	two; apart

Example

di- (apart) + gress (to walk, to step) = **digress**

Use Roots and Prefixes Circle the root and any prefix you find in the boldfaced words below. Use roots, prefixes, and context clues to write the meaning of each word. Check your definitions in a dictionary.

1 Without an exercise partner, it's easy to **regress** and stop working out.

_____

2 The goalpost **deflected** the ball, preventing the kicker from scoring.

_____

3 The word *deflect* **precedes** the word *digress* in the dictionary.

_____

4 Anyone who **exceeds** the speed limit can expect a speeding ticket.

_____

5 Wear clothes that **reflect** light when riding a bike in the evening.

_____

6 My brother Deon will **graduate** from high school in June.

_____

7 Coach Demaris believes in the saying "If at first you don't **succeed**, try, try again."

_____

8 Teachers are confident that students will show **progress** in reading and math.

_____

9 As a **reflex**, she closed her eyes just as her picture was taken.

_____

10 The questions forced the politician to **digress** from her prepared speech.

_____

Process the Meanings

WORD LIST

graduate

exceed

reflect

succeed

reflex

regress

precede

deflect

digress

progress

Choose the Correct Word   Write the word from the Word List that belongs in each sentence. Use each word only once.

1 After _____ in the peace talks, the two countries have signed a treaty.

2 In order to _____ in reaching your goal, plan ahead and work hard.

3 Children can _____ to babylike behavior when a new sibling is born.

4 Did the requests for tickets _____ the number of available seats?

5 Despite our efforts, we couldn't _____ the cat from his goal of scratching all the chairs in the house.

Find Synonyms Write the word from the Word List that is a synonym for the underlined words in each sentence below.

6 Did Sam teach himself to cook, or did he <u>get a degree</u> from a culinary school? _____

7 If the taller students <u>go before</u> the shorter ones, they can fill in the back rows first. _____

8 A sneeze is an <u>automatic response</u> to an irritation of the nose.

_____

9 Margot doesn't <u>stray from her purpose</u> when she urges people to vote.

_____

10 The sun's rays that <u>bounce off</u> the water make driving on this road dangerous. _____

Apply What You've Learned

Demonstrate Word Knowledge Answer the questions or follow the directions.

1 Under what circumstances would you not want a speaker to **digress**?

_____

2 What would you like to do after you **graduate** from high school?

_____

3 What could cause a person to **regress**?

_____

4 Tell about something that has **exceeded** your expectations.

_____

5 Describe a mirror using the word **reflect** (with or without an added ending).

_____

6 List two things that could help you **succeed** at something difficult.

_____

7 Describe your **progress** in learning vocabulary so far.

_____

8 Which family member has a birthday that **precedes** yours?

_____

9 In soccer, what can you use to **deflect** the ball?

_____

10 Discuss a job that requires good **reflexes**.

_____

 Speak It! Imagine that you are one hundred years old. Tell about your life. How has the world changed? Use as many words from the Word List in Part 2 as you can.

PART 3

Reference Skills

for Word Wisdom

The Olympic National Park:

A Walk in a Rain Forest

Come with me on a walk through a rain forest. This is not the kind of rain forest you might expect. This rain forest is not in the steamy tropics. It's a temperate rain forest in cool Washington State, which receives about 150 inches of rain a year, compared to 400 inches in a tropical rain forest. Still, you had better wear your raincoat.

We're going to **amble** through the Quinault Rain Forest. It's in the southern part of the Olympic National Park. This forest borders the Pacific coast for 1,200 miles. It stretches from Oregon to Alaska.

A temperate rain forest has fewer species than a tropical rain forest, but its trees are much older than those in the tropics. A temperate rain forest might contain only ten to twenty kinds of trees, and most of those trees would have needles. Tropical rain forests have hundreds of species of trees, and most of them have broad leaves. The trees in temperate forests are 500 to 1,000 years old, but those in tropical forests are only fifty to one hundred years old.

Although temperate rain forests receive less rain, they also obtain moisture from the coastal fog that **diffuses** among the trees. The air is full of a fine mist, and water drips from the trees. Still, we won't let that **deter** us from hiking through this forest. It's about sixty-five degrees today, but the temperature can **fluctuate** from eighty degrees on the hottest days of summer to just above freezing on the coldest days of winter.

As we walk through the cool shade, huge conifer trees tower as high as 300 feet above us. The trunk of one enormous tree near the trail must be one hundred feet around. The tree's thick, rough bark helps keep moisture from evaporating from its trunk. High above us are *lianas,* vines that climb up taller plants so they can reach the sunlight. The roots of the *lianas* **cascade** down to the ground from high tree branches. By climbing up to the sunlight, the *lianas* have **evolved** and adapted so they can flourish in the rain forest.

The rain forest is full of other forms of life, too. You kick over a rock, and a millipede runs out. Strange but fascinating, millipedes help recycle rotting plants so they can become food for more plants. When I touch the millipede lightly with a stick, it rolls into a ball. These creatures **compress** their bodies into a tight ball and let their shell protect them. When threatened, they can also **eject** a cyanide scent that is poisonous to insects and other small predators.

Suddenly it's raining, so you had better pull up your hood or **deploy** your umbrella. Wow! If it rains much harder, we might have to **evacuate** the forest and end our walk! But the rain stops as quickly as it started. Rays of sun slip through the canopy overhead. What a great day for a walk!

Practice the Context Clues Strategy Here are two of the boldfaced words from the essay on page 106. Use the context clues strategy you learned in Part 1 on page 95 to figure out the meanings of these words.

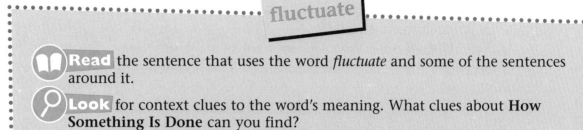

Read the sentence that uses the word *fluctuate* and some of the sentences around it.

Look for context clues to the word's meaning. What clues about **How Something Is Done** can you find?

_____

Think about the context clues and other information you already know.

_____

Predict a meaning for the word *fluctuate*.

_____

Check your Word Wisdom Dictionary to be sure of the meaning of the word *fluctuate*. Write the definition here.

_____

compress

Read the sentence that uses the word *compress* and some of the sentences around it.

Look for context clues to the word's meaning. What clues about **How Something Is Done** can you find?

_____

Think about the context clues and other information you already know.

_____

Predict a meaning for the word *compress*.

_____

Check your Word Wisdom Dictionary to be sure of the meaning of the word *compress*. Which of the meanings for the word *compress* fits the context?

_____

🔑 Unlock the Meanings

Judging Web Pages The Internet contains a lot of information. How can you tell if the information is useful and reliable? Ask yourself these questions:

- Is the URL (the Internet address) that of a school, business, nonprofit group, or a government department? School URLs end with *.edu*. Those of nonprofit groups usually end with *.org*. Business URLs end with *.com*. Government URLs end with *.gov*.
- Who wrote the information on the Web site? Is that person knowledgeable and qualified to write the information?
- Are sources of facts shown? Are they up-to-date?
- Is the sponsor of the page named? Is there a way to contact that sponsor?

Use Internet Reference Skills Underline the best answer to each question.

1 Based on its URL, which Web site would be more likely to explain how a **cascade** is formed?

    a. www.watercascade.com   b. www.watercascade.edu

2 Based on its URL, which Web site would be more likely to sell you bottled water from a certain **cascade**?

    a. www.watercascade.org   b. www.watercascade.com

3 Based on its URL, which Web site would be most likely to have information about efforts to **deter** breaking clean-water laws?

    a. www.watercascade.gov   b. www.watercascade.com

4 Which Web site would give more reliable information about how light is **diffused**?

    a. one sponsored by a sixth-grade student

    b. one sponsored by a sixth-grade science teacher

5 Where are you more likely to learn about how horse training has **evolved**?

    a. a Web site sponsored by a nonprofit group for horse rescue

    b. a Web site sponsored by a horse-training school

Find the Meaning

1. Use context clues.
2. Look for a familiar root, prefix, or suffix.
3. If the context or a word part doesn't help, check the dictionary.

WORD LIST

amble

diffuse

deter

fluctuate

cascade

evolve

compress

eject

deploy

evacuate

Define the Words   Follow the steps above to write the meaning of each boldfaced word. Then write 1, 2, or 3 to show which steps you used.

1 I can **compress** this four-page story into two pages.

_____

2 The students **ambled** through the woods, examining leaves, berries, and flowers.

_____

3 One spray from the air freshener bottle **diffused** the fragrance throughout the house.

_____

4 The water **cascaded** over hundreds of rocks to the river below.

_____

5 The president **deployed** troops to the island to keep the peace.

_____

6 Does your mood **fluctuate** as often and as quickly as the weather?

_____

7 The candies are cooled, wrapped, and **ejected** automatically into bags.

_____

8 Over time, your writing style and voice tend to change and **evolve**.

_____

9 You must **evacuate** the house if the fire alarm goes off.

_____

10 The sign "Beware of Cat" won't **deter** anyone from going into the garden.

_____

Process the Meanings

WORD LIST

amble

diffuse

deter

fluctuate

cascade

evolve

compress

eject

deploy

evacuate

Use the Words Correctly in Writing Rewrite each sentence in your own words. Include the word in parentheses. You may add an ending to the word.

1 Ian's temperature changed from normal to high and back to normal. (fluctuate)

_____

2 The manager warned that we would be thrown out of the theater for whistling. (eject)

_____

3 People had to leave their homes because the brush fires were advancing. (evacuate)

_____

4 I can't believe that this sleeping bag squeezes to fit into that tiny sack! (compress)

_____

5 Jason's sprained ankle will not keep him from playing in the final match. (deter)

_____

6 Amy's red hair fell over her shoulders like a waterfall. (cascade)

_____

7 My dogs race around the yard; they never walk around slowly. (amble)

_____

8 Troops were put in position to guard the leaders during the important meeting. (deploy)

_____

9 If we give it time, the plan for improving our grades will develop. (evolve)

_____

10 The light coming through the frosted window was spread throughout the room. (diffuse)

_____

Apply What You've Learned

Answer the Questions Use what you have learned about each boldfaced word to answer each question. Write **yes** or **no** on the line and explain your answer.

1 Would you expect a trickle of water from a hose to **cascade**?

_____

2 Could a player who loses his temper be **ejected** from a game?

_____

3 Do volunteers need a leader to **deploy** them to a project?

_____

4 After the danger is over, should people **evacuate** the area?

_____

5 Could a tall fence **deter** deer from eating the plants in a garden?

_____

6 Do things that move in a circle, such as a carousel, **evolve**?

_____

7 Do competitors in a race **amble** toward the finish line?

_____

8 Can you **compress** a dozen baseballs into a tiny paper bag?

_____

9 When baking, would you **diffuse** sugar to double a recipe?

_____

10 Can a person's appetite **fluctuate**?

_____

Write It! Write a story about a day in your life. Include the theme of Movement. Use as many words from the Word List in Part 3 as you can.

Review

for Word Wisdom

Sort by Categories   Sort the words in the Word List by categories. Write the word in the correct section of the chart. The number by each head tells how many words should be in that section.

WORD LIST

surmount

initiate

impede

paralyze

proceed

gradual

marshal

resume

flexible

relinquish

graduate

exceed

reflect

succeed

reflex

regress

precede

deflect

digress

progress

amble

diffuse

deter

fluctuate

cascade

evolve

compress

eject

deploy

evacuate

Words about stopping (5)

Words about starting (4)

Words about changing (7)

Words about moving or going (15)

Choose the Correct Word Read each sentence and the two words in parentheses. Circle the word that makes sense in the sentence.

1 Bruno won't (evolve, relinquish) the dog he has raised from a puppy.

2 As a (reflex, progress), Heidi's hands shot out in front of her to break her fall.

3 Rain (reflected, cascaded) from the roof and lashed against the windows.

4 Some people use humor to (deflect, deploy) negative comments.

5 Grandma had to (compress, marshal) her strength to bake three pies for Thanksgiving.

6 After a month of mastering cartwheels, Adam (impeded, graduated) to back flips.

7 Did Louisa May Alcott's book *Little Men* (precede, proceed) *Little Women*?

8 By stringing leaves and flowers on (gradual, flexible) wire, Meredith made a wreath.

9 The city (deployed, resumed) a crew to clean up the streets after the parade.

10 It can be difficult to (amble, initiate) conversation in a group of strangers.

11 After the initial work was done, we were ready to (regress, progress) to the next part of the project.

12 Thick underbrush and wet soil were enough to (impede, deter) our hike through the woods.

13 A dozen candles (reflected, diffused) a soft glow throughout the room.

14 Vera (graduated, ambled) through the garden, admiring the lovely flowers and majestic trees.

15 The snake's venom (paralyzed, reflected) its prey.

Taking Vocabulary Tests

TEST-TAKING STRATEGY

Neatness counts—even on multiple-choice tests. Some tests are scored by machine. Machines may pick up stray marks as answers. They may skip a partially filled circle. For these reasons, be sure to darken the answer circle completely. Check to see that you have erased completely when you change your mind about an answer.

Sample:

Fill in the circle for the word that means the OPPOSITE of the boldfaced word in each phrase.

succeed at the task

O accomplish
O rebel
O question
● fail

Practice Test   Fill in the circle for the word that means the OPPOSITE of the boldfaced word in each phrase.

1 gradual improvement
O immediate
O impressive
O easy
O mixed

2 eject the cartridge
O dismiss
O compare
O insert
O spin

3 impede the investigation
O advertise
O ignore
O cancel
O help

4 evacuate the building
O calm
O fill
O poll
O compliment

5 compress the data
O check
O investigate
O expand
O use

6 surmount the difficulties
O give up
O think about
O compare with
O prefer to

7 proceed to the crosswalk
O go
O plan
O change
O move away from

8 diffuse the seeds
O scatter
O gather
O toss
O combine

9 paralyze the effort
O strengthen
O teach
O freeze
O communicate

10 resume reading
O enjoy
O continue
O end
O avoid

Build New Words

Use Suffixes to Turn Verbs Into Adjectives The suffixes -*able* and -*ible*, which mean "able to be," turn verbs into adjectives. Use the suffixes -*able* and -*ible* to turn the following verbs from the Word List into adjectives. You will have to change the spelling of one word. Check the Word Wisdom Dictionary if you're not sure of the spelling. Then, use the new adjectives to write sentences.

Word	+ Suffix	= Adjective	Sentence
surmount	-able		_____ _____
diffuse	-ible		_____ _____
deploy	-able		_____ _____
compress	-ible		_____ _____
eject	-able		_____ _____

Speak It! Give a speech about the importance of moving and exercise. Use as many words from this Movement unit as you can.

Context Clues

for Word Wisdom

Wisdom That Lives On:
Confucius

Confucius was known by only a few people during his lifetime. Yet today, he is often regarded as one of the most influential people who ever lived. His ideas are still alive after twenty-five centuries.

Confucius was born about 551 B.C. in northeastern China. His father died when Confucius was three years old, and the family was poor. In ancient times, only boys of wealthy families were educated. Somehow, though, Confucius managed to learn. By the age of fifteen, he knew that he wanted to study for the rest of his life. He began to teach others when he was twenty-one years old. As a **deferential** gesture toward him, his students called him "Master."

Confucius was a philosopher. He thought more deeply than most people about the meaning of life. This **sage** thinker was concerned with behavior and relationships. Civilization, he thought, was collapsing around him. Unless people became more **humane** rather than being cruel to each other, China would experience great suffering. Confucius believed that people could live in **harmony** and not in disagreement. Those in power could promote the well-being of their subjects. Ordinary people could go out of their way to treat one another kindly. Everyone could have a shared sense of

loyalty. Both rich and poor could feel an **obligation** to care for one another instead of thinking that they had no responsibilities toward their fellow human beings.

At the center of Confucius's philosophy was a love for humanity. Whether an **acquaintance,** family member, or friend, everyone deserves courtesy and respect. Practice **generosity** instead of greed, said Confucius. Strive for cooperation instead of rivalry. Harmony can be found in the **rituals** that express society's shared values. These are what hold a family or a nation together, Confucius taught.

Confucius never **attained** a position of authority. He never got a chance to reform government practices. He did, however, make a difference. We are all **heirs** to his philosophy. His influence lives on in many of our ideas and documents. His effect is felt in the classroom when students question ideas and think for themselves. His wise sayings guide us toward better behavior. His dreams of a world improved by human goodness become our dreams.

Context Clues Strategy

Look for Antonyms

EXAMPLE: There was *enmity*, not warm friendship, among the committee members.

CLUE: The word *not* indicates a contrast or a difference. The phrase *warm friendship* is what *enmity* is *not*. Warm friendship is the antonym of *enmity*.

Here are the steps for using this context clues strategy to figure out the meaning of the word *obligation*, which appears in the essay you just read.

Read the sentence that uses the unknown word and some of the sentences around it.

*Everyone could have a shared sense of loyalty. Both rich and poor could feel an **obligation** to care for one another instead of thinking that they had no responsibilities toward their fellow human beings.*

Look for context clues. What **Antonyms** of the word *obligation* can you find?

The phrase *instead of* signals an antonym. The phrase *no responsibilities* is opposite in meaning to the word *obligation*.

Think about the context clues and other helpful information you already know.

Confucius wanted people to be kind to one another. I've heard the word *obligation* before. People sometimes use it when they talk about doing something for someone else.

Predict a meaning for the word.

Obligation must mean "responsibility."

Check a dictionary to be sure of the meaning of *obligation*.

The word *obligation* means "responsibility; a sense of duty."

🔒 Unlock the Meanings

Practice the Strategy Here are two of the boldfaced words from the essay about Confucius. Use the context clues strategy on page 117 to figure out the meaning of each word.

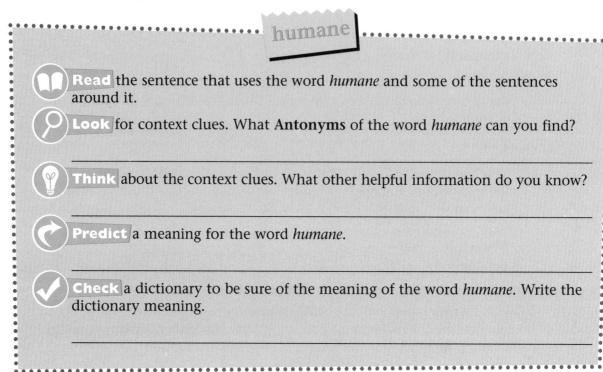

humane

📖 **Read** the sentence that uses the word *humane* and some of the sentences around it.

🔍 **Look** for context clues. What **Antonyms** of the word *humane* can you find?

_____

💡 **Think** about the context clues. What other helpful information do you know?

_____

➡️ **Predict** a meaning for the word *humane*.

_____

✔️ **Check** a dictionary to be sure of the meaning of the word *humane*. Write the dictionary meaning.

_____

harmony

📖 **Read** the sentence that uses the word *harmony* and some of the sentences around it.

🔍 **Look** for context clues. What **Antonyms** of the word *harmony* can you find?

_____

💡 **Think** about the context clues. What other helpful information do you know?

_____

➡️ **Predict** a meaning for the word *harmony*.

_____

✔️ **Check** your Word Wisdom Dictionary to be sure of the meaning of *harmony*. Which of the meanings fits the context?

_____

Use Context Clues You have been introduced to three words from the essay on page 116. These words are checked off in the Word List. In the first column, write the other seven words from the Word List. In the second column, predict a meaning for each word using context clues. Then look up the meaning of the word in a dictionary. In the third column, write the dictionary meaning that fits the context.

WORD LIST
deferential
sage
✔ humane
✔ harmony
✔ obligation
acquaintance
generosity
ritual
attain
heir

	Vocabulary Word	Your Prediction	Dictionary Says
1			
2			
3			
4			
5			
6			
7			

Process the Meanings

WORD LIST

deferential

sage

humane

harmony

obligation

acquaintance

generosity

ritual

attain

heir

Choose the Correct Words Write the word from the Word List that best completes each sentence. You will need to add an ending to some words.

1 Eighty-year-old Grandma Moses _____ recognition for her paintings and proved that it is never too late to begin creative work.

2 Several science and math scholarships were funded by the _____ of the officers of the computer company.

3 Forgotten Felines is an organization dedicated to the rescue and _____ treatment of abandoned cats.

4 _____ to kingdoms spend their childhood years preparing for their future roles as kings or queens.

5 The team relied on Coach Sparks for his _____ advice about training, nutrition, and technique.

6 One way to fulfill your community service _____ is to help clean up a local park.

7 In my family, the first day of school is marked every year by the _____ of having a big breakfast together.

8 Story time is an effective way to bring _____ to a busy and restless kindergarten class.

9 Having moved to a new school only six months ago, Josh had more _____ than close friends.

10 The _____ gesture of standing when a lady enters the room seems to have gone out of style.

Apply What You've Learned

Demonstrate Word Knowledge   Complete the following sentences.

1 It might take time to trust an **acquaintance** because

_____

2 One example of **deferential** behavior is _____

_____

3 An act of **generosity** I could do is _____

_____

4 One goal I would like to **attain** is _____

_____

5 An **obligation** I can't avoid is _____

Use the Words Correctly   Complete the sentences by choosing the phrase that best explains the boldfaced word. Write the letter of your choice on the blank line.

_____ **6** **Humane** acts are likely to

   a. make people feel bad.   b. be satisfying and rewarding.

_____ **7** A practice becomes a **ritual** when it

   a. is repeated in a set pattern.   b. is abandoned altogether.

_____ **8** A person who is **heir** to the throne will

   a. some day be the ruler.   b. go into the military.

_____ **9** **Sage** ideas come from people who

   a. are eager to be helpful.   b. have wisdom and good judgment.

_____ **10** **Harmony** among club members is achieved by

   a. making agreements that work for all.   b. letting one person control all decisions.

Write It!   Confucius said, "I am fortunate indeed. Whenever I make a mistake, there is always someone to notice it." Explain what you think this means. Give an example from your own experience. Use as many vocabulary words from Part 1 as you can.

PART 2 Latin and Greek Roots

for Word Wisdom

The Personality Debate:
Nature or Nurture?

Do you think you were born with your personality? Or did your environment shape you? Is your behavior determined by nature—the genes you were born with? Or is your behavior determined by nurture—what you have learned?

Scientists agree that we gain many physical characteristics through **heredity**. Genes for eye color, hair color, height, and so on are passed from one **generation** to another. Let's say your **inheritance** from your parents includes two dominant genes for brown eyes. Then you will have brown eyes, too. Some families can trace physical characteristics, such as red hair, through their **genealogy**.

At the same time, scientists disagree about the source of personality, behavior, and intelligence. Some believe the source is nature: Our genes control our personality and so on. Other scientists believe the source is nurture: We learn to behave in certain ways. Based on the nurture theory, one **gender** plays with dolls because it learns to do so. The other gender learns to play with trucks.

Those who believe the nature theory point to pairs of identical twins who grew up apart. These twins have the same genes. Even with different sets of parents, they tend to have the same kind of personality. In one study, two twins, raised apart, took the same personality test. They scored the same as if one person had taken the test twice.

Another study compared children from wealthy and working-class homes. It found that as long as parents were supportive and loving, they did not influence their **progeny's** intelligence. Private schools and special lessons could not make children smarter. Their intelligence was not learned, but instead **inherited.**

The nurture scientists point out that identical twins reared apart should be *exactly* the same. After all, they inherit exactly the same genes. However, these twins have learned to be different in some ways. Other studies show that some personality traits can be learned. For example, people can learn to have a sense of humor. Their families and cultures teach them to look for the humor in life.

Many experts now say that our genes do not control us. They do push us in a certain direction, but we can push back. We can find ways to overcome shyness. We can channel aggressiveness into safe activities. We can enroll an awkward child in a baseball **league** or gymnastic lessons. Our personalities are not shaped just by the genes we inherit or just by what we learn. They are shaped by a sort of **alliance** between nature and nurture.

We are **obliged** to these scientists for helping us learn more about ourselves. Perhaps some day they will identify specific genes that push us in a certain direction. Then we can be ready to go in that direction—or to push back.

Practice the Context Clues Strategy   Here are two of the boldfaced words from the essay on page 122. Use the context clues strategy you learned in Part 1 on page 117 to figure out the meanings of these words.

inherited

📖 **Read** the sentence that uses the word *inherited* and some of the sentences around it.

🔍 **Look** for context clues to the word's meaning. What **Antonyms** of the word *inherited* can you find?

_____

💡 **Think** about the context clues. What other information do you know?

_____

➡️ **Predict** a meaning for the word *inherit*.

_____

✔️ **Check** your Word Wisdom Dictionary to be sure of the meaning of *inherit*. Which of the meanings for *inherit* fits the context?

_____

alliance

📖 **Read** the sentence that uses the word *alliance* and some of the sentences around it.

🔍 **Look** for context clues to the word's meaning. What **Antonyms** of the word *alliance* can you find?

_____

💡 **Think** about the context clues. What other information do you know?

_____

➡️ **Predict** a meaning for the word *alliance*.

_____

✔️ **Check** your Word Wisdom Dictionary to be sure of the meaning of the word *alliance*. Write the definition here.

_____

🔑 Unlock the Meanings

Several words you studied in Part 1 have Latin or Greek roots. Knowing the meaning of these roots can help you unlock the meaning of many unfamiliar words. Each root has something to do with relationships.

Latin Root: **heir, her**

meaning: an heir

English word: *heir*

meaning: a person who receives ideas from someone who lived earlier

Latin and Greek Root: **gen**

meaning: a kind; to beget

English word: *generosity*

meaning: the willingness to give or share

Latin Root: **lig**

meaning: to bind

English word: *obligation*

meaning: responsibility; a sense of duty

WORD LIST

- heredity
- generation
- inheritance
- genealogy
- gender
- progeny
- inherit
- league
- alliance
- oblige

Categorize by Roots Find these roots in the Word List. Write each word in the correct column. Remember that the spelling of roots can change. Think of other words you know that come from the same roots. Write each word in the correct place.

Latin Root: **heir, her**

Latin and Greek Root: **gen**

Latin Root: **lig**

_____ _____ _____

_____ _____ _____

_____ _____ _____

_____ _____ _____

_____ _____ _____

Relationships

Prefix	Meaning	Example
al-	to, toward	al- (to) + lig (bind) + -ance (noun) = alliance

Use Roots and Prefixes Circle the root and any prefix you find in the boldfaced words below. Use roots, prefixes, and context clues to write the meaning of each boldfaced word. Remember that the spelling of roots can change. Check your definitions in a dictionary.

1 James **inherited** a pocket watch from his great-grandfather.

_____

2 Names that aren't specific in **gender**, such as Jordan and Taylor, are popular.

_____

3 The first baseball **league** for boys started in 1939.

_____

4 Some people can trace their **genealogy** back to the Pilgrims.

_____

5 The parents of the quintuplets gathered their **progeny** for the portrait.

_____

6 We were **obliged** to our neighbors for inviting us to dinner when we moved into the neighborhood.

_____

7 During World War I, many countries formed an **alliance** against the Central Powers.

_____

8 We look like our parents and have some of their talents because of **heredity**.

_____

_____

9 There were four **generations** of relatives at my father's birthday party.

_____

10 Marlene learned that she would have to share her **inheritance** with her mother's dogs.

_____

Process the Meanings

WORD LIST

- heredity
- generation
- inheritance
- genealogy
- gender
- progeny
- inherit
- league
- alliance
- oblige

Choose the Correct Words Write the word from the Word List that best completes each sentence. You will need to add an ending to one word.

1 Styles change with each _____, so a daughter may not want to wear her mother's wedding gown.

2 When people study their _____, the names of family members are written on a picture of a tree.

3 Do you think someone's skill in music or painting comes from education, _____, or both?

4 Much _____ for frequent rides home, Tanya knitted Danielle a scarf to thank her.

5 Before 1970, newspaper job ads started with a _____ label, so that men and women would know which jobs to apply for.

Use the Words Correctly in Writing Rewrite each sentence in your own words. Use the word in parentheses in your sentence. You may need to change one word ending.

6 The three towns formed a group to work for economic progress. (alliance)

_____

7 George got his creativity and a flair for drama from his mother. (inherit)

_____

8 Many people regret wasting the money left to them by an ancestor. (inheritance)

_____

9 As a new artist, Arlene joined an association for people in the same field. (league)

_____

10 *Cheaper by the Dozen* is a story about two parents with twelve children. (progeny)

_____

Apply What You've Learned

Answer the Questions Answer the questions. Explain your answers.

1 Are you a member of the same **generation** as your grandmother?

_____

2 Would someone's **progeny** include aunts, uncles, and cousins?

_____

3 Does **gender** apply to both men and women?

_____

4 Are there situations in which people feel **obliged** to others?

_____

5 Can everyone expect to receive an **inheritance**?

_____

6 Would software for drawing a family tree be helpful to someone interested in **genealogy**?

_____

_____

7 Do best friends who are not related share the same **heredity**?

_____

8 If you **inherit** something, do you have to return it when you're finished with it?

_____

9 Can one person be considered a **league**?

_____

10 Are people who have no interests in common likely to form an **alliance**?

_____

Speak It!   Tell a story about your family or an imaginary family. Use as many vocabulary words from Part 2 as you can.

PART 3 Reference Skills

for Word Wisdom

Pride and Prey: The Social Lion

Lions are among the most ferocious of animals—and the most social. Living together in prides, they rely on each other for food and for the protection of themselves, their cubs, and their territory.

A lion pride can be as small as three individuals or as large as forty. A pride may have one male or up to seven males who work together. The females have a deep **commitment** to their pride. They often live in the same pride for life, while the adult males may stay for only two to four years. After that, they leave on their own, or they are driven off as a stronger male takes over.

In a **traditional** pride, the lionesses do eighty-five to ninety percent of the hunting, while the lions are responsible for patrolling the territory and protecting the pride. Although the males sleep or rest sixteen to twenty hours a day, they still get "the lion's share" of the **communal** meal. They eat first, followed by the lionesses, and then the cubs. The lionesses often work together to chase down and kill their prey. This teamwork ensures that the pride does not go hungry and all members receive a **decent** meal. Their prey ranges from mice to zebras to buffalo.

When the pride is resting, the **rapport** is obvious. Lions are very affectionate toward other members of their pride. They like being together and touch, lick, and rub each other, often with much purring.

When a new lion takes over a pride, however, he often kills all the cubs. He has a clear purpose and is not **apologetic**. He kills the cubs to make sure that he is the father of all future cubs. The mothers try to defend their cubs, but they usually are unsuccessful. The females in a pride all tend to give birth about the same time of the year, have two or three cubs each, and often nurse each other's cubs. This **informal** relationship offers cubs a better chance at survival, especially those born to a weak or sick lioness. Cub mortality is very high, and less than half will survive their first year.

Female cubs will stay with the pride, but males stay only until they are mature, at age five or six. Then they go off on their own, hunting for themselves until they are strong enough to take over a pride. Some lions never find a new pride. They manage to **alienate** others of their kind and wander their whole lives. These lone males receive no **hospitality** from the prides they encounter. The head of the pride quickly drives them off.

Faced with an attacker, however, the head of the pride has many **supporters**. Both males and females fiercely defend their pride from outsiders. They would rather share their kills with pride members than with strangers. After all, the strangers will not be around to help defend them from predators or to help them find food when prey is scarce. For lions, family counts!

Practice the Context Clues Strategy Here are two of the boldfaced words from the essay on page 128. Use the context clues strategy you learned in Part 1 on page 117 to figure out the meanings of these words.

decent

📖 **Read** the sentence that uses the word *decent* and some of the sentences around it.

🔍 **Look** for context clues to the word's meaning. What **Antonyms** of *decent* can you find?

_____

💡 **Think** about the context clues. What other information do you know?

_____

➡️ **Predict** a meaning for the word *decent*.

_____

✔️ **Check** your Word Wisdom Dictionary to be sure of the meaning of the word *decent*. Which of the meanings for the word fits the context?

_____

supporter

📖 **Read** the sentence that uses the word *supporter* and some of the sentences around it.

🔍 **Look** for context clues to the word's meaning. What **Antonyms** of *supporter* can you find?

_____

💡 **Think** about the context clues. What other information do you know?

_____

➡️ **Predict** a meaning for the word *supporter*.

_____

✔️ **Check** your Word Wisdom Dictionary to be sure of the meaning of the word *supporter*. Write the definition here.

_____

Unlock the Meanings

Thesaurus A thesaurus lists synonyms or approximate synonyms. A thesaurus can help you find the perfect word, but you have to pick the right word for the context. A thesaurus in book form is organized alphabetically, like a dictionary, or by ideas. In such a thesaurus, the index at the back of the book will tell you on which page you will find the word and its synonyms.

Computer word-processing software usually has a built-in thesaurus. Highlight the word for which you want a synonym. Then go to the "Tools" menu and open the thesaurus. It will list synonyms for your highlighted word.

Choose the Synonyms Read the sentence and the synonyms for the boldfaced word. The definition of each synonym is given in parentheses. Write the letter of the best synonym for the boldfaced word.

_____ **1** "Was I humming out loud?" He was **apologetic** and embarrassed.
   a. remorseful (filled with bitter guilt)   b. regretful (feeling sorry about)

_____ **2** The girls had a **rapport** based on their interest in chemistry.
   a. agreement (harmony of opinion)   b. relationship (connection)

_____ **3** The invitation said to wear "**informal** clothes—jeans and a T-shirt."
   a. unofficial (lacking authority)   b. casual (not dressed up)

Replace the Words Use a thesaurus to replace the boldfaced words with vivid and descriptive synonyms. Rewrite the sentences.

4 The trip was a **great** experience.

_____

5 Tina read an **interesting** book.

_____

6 Frank is a **nice** person.

_____

7 **8** The brothers had a **long talk**.

_____

9 **10** Lexie **hit** the ball **hard**.

_____

Find the Meaning

1. Use context clues.
2. Look for a familiar root, prefix, or suffix.
3. If the context or a word part doesn't help, check the dictionary.

WORD LIST

commitment

traditional

communal

decent

rapport

apologetic

informal

alienate

hospitality

supporter

Define the Words   Follow the steps above to write the meaning of each boldfaced word. Write 1, 2, or 3 to show which steps you used.

1 Bob made a **commitment** to study every day, not just before the test.

_____

2 Everyone drew water from the **communal** well in the center of the village.

_____

3 His bad attitude and hostility began to **alienate** even those closest to him.

_____

4 During rehearsals, a warm **rapport** developed among the cast members.

_____

5 As the candidate swept into the room, her **supporters** rose to their feet and applauded.

_____

6 It was **decent** of the Durbans to lend us their sleeping bags and tent.

_____

7 The Diaz family is known for their **hospitality**; they often invite guests to their home.

_____

8 If she thought before speaking, she wouldn't have to be so **apologetic** for her remarks.

_____

9 The casual open studios are **informal** places where people can meet artists.

_____

10 The polka is a lively **traditional** dance that has been enjoyed for centuries.

_____

Process the Meanings

WORD LIST

- commitment
- traditional
- communal
- decent
- rapport
- apologetic
- informal
- alienate
- hospitality
- supporter

Choose the Correct Words   Write the word from the Word List that best fits in each group of words with similar meanings.

1 public, shared, common, _____

2 kind, generous, thoughtful, _____

3 customary, usual, established, _____

4 withdraw, oppose, separate, _____

5 vow, guarantee, pledge, _____

Use the Words Correctly in Writing   Rewrite each sentence in your own words. Include the word in parentheses. You may add an ending to some words.

6 Her followers signed a petition to nominate her for the presidency. (supporter)

_____

_____

7 How can we ever thank you for the welcome you showed us during our visit? (hospitality)

_____

_____

8 Despite the casual tone, everyone understood the seriousness of the discussion. (informal)

_____

_____

9 He sounded very sorry for dropping his piece of pie on my shoe. (apologetic)

_____

_____

10 Although they were related, they didn't seem to have a good connection. (rapport)

_____

_____

Apply What You've Learned

Solve the Riddles   Write the word from the Word List that matches each clue.

1 This is something that good hosts offer their guests. _____

2 This could describe a swimming pool in an apartment building.

_____

3 This is what people feel when they like each other. _____

4 This kind of note could help a person get over hurt feelings.

_____

5 It could be irresponsible or inconsiderate to break this.

_____

6 Someone who agrees with a recycling plan might be called this.

_____

Demonstrate Word Knowledge   Answer the questions or follow the directions.

7 What are two **informal** things you do that you really enjoy?

_____

8 Explain why you think your parents are modern or **traditional** in their thinking.

_____

9 If you **alienate** a friend, what could you do to make up for it?

_____

10 What is one **decent** thing a person has done for you?

_____

Write It!   Describe a relationship you have with someone. It could be someone you have been best friends with for a long time or someone you met recently. Use as many vocabulary words from Part 3 as you can.

Review

for Word Wisdom

Categorize by Parts of Speech Categorize the words in the Word List by part of speech. Write each word in the correct column. The numbers tell you how many words to list in each column. Then circle the words that have the roots *heir, her, gen,* and *lig.*

WORD LIST

- deferential
- sage
- humane
- harmony
- obligation
- acquaintance
- generosity
- ritual
- attain
- heir
- heredity
- generation
- inheritance
- genealogy
- gender
- progeny
- inherit
- league
- alliance
- oblige
- commitment
- traditional
- communal
- decent
- rapport
- apologetic
- informal
- alienate
- hospitality
- supporter

Nouns 18	Verbs 4	Adjectives 8

Choose the Correct Words Write the words from the box where they belong in the paragraph below.

gender	informal	genealogy
progeny	heredity	generation

If you're interested in your roots, you may want to study your family's

1 _____. That study won't give you details about your

specific **2** _____, such as body type or musical ability.

With some research, though, you can find out about every

3 _____ that came before yours and the

4 _____ of all of their **5** _____.

There are many resources available to you, from **6** _____

interviews you can have with your own relatives to more standard sources, such

as U.S. census records, military archives, and the files of local historical societies.

Answer the Questions Circle the vocabulary word that best answers each question.

7 What kind of advice would you get from a wise person? (sage, apologetic)

8 Who would rule after a king dies? (acquaintance, heir)

9 Which adjective suggests that a custom has been in someone's family for many generations? (communal, traditional)

10 Which word describes the behavior of a visitor toward a respected leader? (deferential, traditional)

11 What is a repeated ceremony called? (league, ritual)

12 What describes someone who feels guilty? (apologetic, communal)

13 What should co-workers try to develop? (gender, rapport)

14 What would a politician try to get? (supporters, generations)

15 What do you do when you try hard to get something? (oblige, attain)

Review

Taking Vocabulary Tests

Sample:

Every culture has _____ for celebrating birthdays. In China, for example, a child's first birthday is marked by a ceremony in which he or she is surrounded by objects. The Chinese believe that the object the baby chooses indicates the child's future. On his twelfth birthday, a Sikh boy in India learns to wrap his turban. Then the boy gets presents from his _____ and others who wish him well.

Ⓐ rituals, supporters
Ⓑ obligations, heirs
Ⓒ generations, alliances
Ⓓ inheritance, commitments

Practice Test   Fill in the letter of the word or words that best complete each paragraph.

1   Since colonial days, the pineapple has been a symbol of _____. Sea captains placed the fruit, brought from the West Indies, outside their doors as a sign that they had returned from a voyage. The pineapple was an invitation for visitors to stop by. Today, doors, shutters, and even fence posts are decorated with the pineapple to show that the house is a place of welcome and good cheer.

Ⓐ obligation
Ⓑ league
Ⓒ hospitality
Ⓓ acquaintance

2   At the end of World War I, President Woodrow Wilson wanted to make the world safe for democracy. To do this, he suggested that the United States, Great Britain, France, and Russia form a(n) _____ of nations that would protect one another's territory and independence. Wilson thought this was a sure way to achieve world peace, because countries would be _____ to each other for this help. However, Americans didn't want to get involved in other countries' conflicts and refused to join. The League of Nations collapsed in 1939.

Ⓐ commitment, alienated
Ⓑ alliance, obliged
Ⓒ generosity, inherited
Ⓓ supporter, attained

3   Dr. McCloskey has a great bedside manner. She is always calm and comforting. A smile often crinkles the corners of her eyes. She listens as if her patients' words are the only thing that matters. She has a wonderful _____ with every patient, no matter what the patient's age or condition is. She is the most _____ doctor I know.

Ⓐ acquaintance, alienated
Ⓑ obligation, sage
Ⓒ rapport, humane
Ⓓ alliance, apologetic

Play with Language

Find the Words The words from the box below are hidden in the puzzle. They go in all directions. Circle them as you find them.

acquaintance	attain	generosity	alienate
obligation	rapport	communal	league
commitment	decent	inheritance	humane

```
N R F M L H B R A C K I S H S
O S A E A O R U C R I G U A R
B I R S K P L I Q U N O R M E
R O M S E L A N U M M O C M N
S O D R H S C J A B G E H O G
S M E O E T U U I L L P A C I
A R L O R R Z S N R Y I R K S
T A E C O M M I T M E N T O E
M N U O R D N O A S A H E A D
O W G G I U O N N R E E D U D
E Z A O S N I S C J T R O T I
N D E C E N T R E C I I P E T
A A L B G R A P P O R T R V N
M D O A R G G U I D E A E E A
U L S L E L I N P U T N O N T
H A T I A A L O R E D C P R U
M D U E T S B S H O M E L T R
I G E N E R O S I T Y S Y O E
L Y V A R I Y I E Y E B R T W
K X A T T A I N K O N G A O R
P E Z E E N A G L A S T I H A
U T R E N G S S B I R D N P P
```

Speak It! Pretend you are a philosopher like Confucius. Discuss your observations on life or human nature. Persuade your audience to think as you do by telling them how your observations will change their lives. Use as many vocabulary words from Part 4 as you can.

PART 1

Context Clues

for Word Wisdom

Earth, Wind, and Fire:
The Art of Glassblowing

As delicate as an egg or a scallop shell, an aquamarine bowl glows like the Caribbean Sea. A golden goblet seems to blaze from within. Some vessels are hollow, as light as cobwebs. Others are weighty and crusty with texture. All seem, somehow, to occupy the impossible space between solid and liquid.

Glassblowing takes a lot of energy, imagination, and skill. Made of earth, formed by breath, and born in fire, blown glass is an astonishing, but difficult, art form.

The process begins as the ingredients of glass—sand, potash, and iron oxide—are melted in a **kiln** at between 2,200 and 2,500 degrees Fahrenheit. At these extreme temperatures, **molten** glass resembles white-hot honey. Using a four-foot-long hollow iron pipe, the artist blows into the **incandescent**, glowing lump. The glassblower controls the size, shape, and thickness of the hollow lump by the amount of air he or she forces into it.

As the glass cools slightly, the artist **manipulates** it much like taffy. The glass can be **elongated** to the desired length as the artist swings the blowpipe. It can also be flattened with **pincers**. The artist uses **calipers** to check the size. To keep the partly finished piece **pliable**, the artist may reheat it frequently. The colorless bubble begins to shine with a beautiful **luster**. The glassblower rolls it across a steel plate sprinkled with colored glass dust. When the glass goes into the kiln again, the color is fused into the glass.

Then comes the controlled cooling stage. The still hot glass goes back into the kiln, where it remains at a constant temperature. Gradually, the heat is reduced. Depending on the size and thickness of the piece, cooling can take hours or even days. If the cooling is done properly, stresses in the glass are reduced to a minimum. Then the piece will be less likely to crack or break.

Skill and coordination are required to gather, shape, and control the glass. Even the tiniest mistake can destroy a piece any time during the process. The artist must be aware of the most **subtle** changes in temperature and balance. This makes the art of glassblowing difficult for most people to master. Yet the process of converting raw materials into a thing of beauty makes the effort worthwhile. Whether the pieces are practical or decorative, they constitute a fine art made of earth, wind, and fire.

Appearance

UNIT 7

Context Clues Strategy

Look for What the Word Is Used For

EXAMPLE: Paula used special metal *shears* to cut the glass bubble in half.

CLUE: The words *to cut the glass bubble in half* tell what *shears* are used for.

One way to understand the meaning of new words is to use the context in which the word appears. The way an unfamiliar word is used with other, more familiar words can give you clues to its meaning. Here are the steps for using this context clues strategy to figure out the meaning of the word *kiln*, which appeared in the essay you just read.

Read the sentence that uses the unknown word and some of the sentences around it.

- - - - -

*The process begins as the ingredients of glass—sand, potash, and iron oxide—are melted in a **kiln** at between 2,200 and 2,500 degrees Fahrenheit.*

Look for context clues. What clues showing **What the Word Is Used For** can you find?

- - - - -

A kiln melts glass ingredients at very high temperatures.

Think about the context clues and other helpful information you already know.

- - - - -

This is something that turns the ingredients of glass into a liquid.

Predict a meaning for the word *kiln*.

- - - - -

A *kiln* must be a furnace for liquefying glass.

Check your Word Wisdom Dictionary to be sure of the meaning.

- - - - -

A *kiln* is a furnace for melting glass or drying clay.

🔓 Unlock the Meanings

Practice the Strategy Here are two of the boldfaced words from the essay on page 138. Use the context clues strategy on page 139 to figure out the meaning of each word.

pincers

📖 **Read** the sentence that uses the word *pincers* and some of the sentences around it.

🔍 **Look** for context clues. What clues showing **What the Word Is Used For** can you find?

_____

💡 **Think** about the context clues. What other helpful information do you know?

_____

➡️ **Predict** a meaning for the word *pincers*.

_____

✔️ **Check** a dictionary to see how it defines the word *pincers*. Which of the meanings for the word fits the context? Write the definition here.

_____

calipers

📖 **Read** the sentence that uses the word *calipers* and some of the sentences around it.

🔍 **Look** for context clues. What clues showing **What the Word Is Used For** can you find?

_____

💡 **Think** about the context clues. What other helpful information do you know?

_____

➡️ **Predict** a meaning for the word *calipers*.

_____

✔️ **Check** a dictionary to be sure of the meaning of the word *calipers*. Write the definition here.

_____

WORD LIST
✔ kiln
molten
incandescent
manipulate
elongate
✔ pincers
✔ calipers
pliable
luster
subtle

Use Context Clues You have been introduced to three vocabulary words from the glassblowing essay. Those words are checked off in the Word List here. In the first column, write the other seven words from the Word List. In the second column, use context to predict a meaning for each word. Then look up the meanings in your Word Wisdom Dictionary. Write the definition in the third column.

Vocabulary Word	Your Prediction	Dictionary Says
1		
2		
3		
4		
5		
6		
7		

Process the Meanings

WORD LIST

- kiln
- molten
- incandescent
- manipulate
- elongate
- pincers
- calipers
- pliable
- luster
- subtle

Choose the Correct Word Write the word from the Word List that best completes each sentence. Use each word only once. You will need to add an ending to one word.

1 The scientist used _____ to grasp the dead beetle's body and gently flatten its thin antennae.

2 The color variation in the glass vase was so _____ that most people didn't realize they were looking at three colors, not one.

3 Candlelight emphasized the gleam of the shining dishes and the _____ of the polished silverware.

4 Everything from head size to amount of body fat can be measured with _____ .

5 Bright orange _____ lava poured down the side of the volcano, burning everything in its path.

6 The Swiss sculptor Alberto Giacometti _____ his wire and plaster people, making them very thin, lengthy, and dreamlike.

7 Some kinds of clay dry out less quickly than others; therefore, they remain _____ longer.

8 Before these unusual bowls can be baked in the _____ , their feet must be coated in wax to keep them from sticking to the shelf.

9 A gas fireplace does not really substitute for a wood-burning fireplace; the _____ glow it provides is fine, but there is no crackle or dance of flames.

10 When he was fifteen years old, Todd learned to _____ the complicated hay baler at his grandfather's farm.

Demonstrate Word Knowledge Use your understanding of the boldfaced vocabulary words to decide whether each statement is true or false. First, write **true** or **false** on the answer line. Then give a reason for your choice.

1 **Incandescent** coals on a barbecue grill are not hot enough for cooking.

_____

2 **Pincers** could be made by folding a strip of sheet steel into a V-shape.

_____

3 Bread and pizza are baked in a **kiln**. _____

_____

4 Dentists need stiff hands to **manipulate** tools inside their patients' mouths.

_____

5 **Molten** hot chocolate will burn your tongue. _____

_____

6 Metals like silver and gold rarely have a **luster**._____

_____

7 **Subtle** changes may slip by those who do not look at things carefully.

_____

8 When you **elongate** something, you stretch it until it is long and thin.

_____

9 Concrete and stone are good flooring materials because they are so **pliable**.

_____

10 **Calipers** are useful in cooking because they measure anything from a teaspoon to a cup.

_____

_____

Write It! Write a publicity article or a brochure for an art exhibit. Let people know where and when they can see the exhibit. Describe a few of the art works. Use as many words from the Word List in Part 1 as you can.

PART 2 Latin Roots

for Word Wisdom

To Glow or Not to Glow:
A Fight Over Fish

Have you seen the new GloFish™? They are genetically altered zebra fish. No longer black and white, the fish glow bright red or green.

Some people object to GloFish because they believe that scientists altered their genes "just for fun." But, the fish were developed by Zhiyuan Gong, a researcher at the National University of Singapore, as a way to detect water pollution. As a result, Gong has become a **luminary** in the field of genetic engineering. He is leading others to consider new uses for genetic changes. Gong's goal is to produce fish that can be used to indicate specific kinds of pollution. For example, green fish would glow in the presence of certain pollutants. Red fish would glow in the presence of other pollutants. Gong has taken a two-**ply** approach to this challenge. First, he learned how to take the glow-genes out of jellyfish and transfer them into the eggs of zebra fish. Now he is working on a way to turn the glow on and off.

The genetically altered zebra fish is now one of many **luminescent** organisms. Deep in the ocean, where sunlight cannot reach, ninety percent of the creatures are luminescent. About half of all jellyfish are luminescent. Some of them glow like **chandeliers** as they float through the water. Some jellyfish can produce bright flashes of light to startle their predators.

Why are so many ocean creatures **lucent**? For some, glowing is a way of finding or attracting prey. The flashlight fish, for example, uses its light to spot tiny, tasty fish. For other creatures, glowing is a form of protection. In parts of the ocean where the sunlight is dim, the water is more **translucent** than clear. There, some creatures use luminescence to make themselves match the color and brightness of the dim sunlight. Then their predators have a hard time locating them.

Probably the most **illustrious** examples of luminescence are fireflies, or lightning bugs. They glow as a form of communication. Male fireflies use flashes of light to attract females.

The **supple** little GloFish certainly brighten up aquariums. Still, some people worry that they will escape into the wild and cause problems. However, these **compliant** little fish are not aggressive or poisonous, and they are as healthy as any other fish.

Most people, however, are not worried about any damage the fish might do. Instead, they are asking **candid** questions about the ethics of changing an organism's genes. What will be next, they ask, blue dogs and green cats?

GloFish have now been banned in California. That state's Fish and Game Commission has refused to allow the fish to be sold. One commissioner said, "To me, this seems like an abuse of the power we have over life, and I'm not prepared to go there today. This is a question of values, not a question of science."

Practice the Context Clues Strategy Here are two of the boldfaced words from the essay on page 144. Use the context clues strategy you learned in Part 1 on page 139 to figure out the meanings of these words.

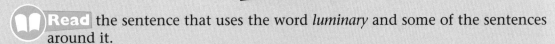

luminary

Read the sentence that uses the word *luminary* and some of the sentences around it.

Look for context clues to the word's meaning. What clues showing **What the Word Is Used For** can you find?

_____

_____

Think about the context clues and other information you already know.

_____

Predict a meaning for the word *luminary*.

_____

Check your Word Wisdom Dictionary to be sure of the meaning of the word *luminary*. Which of the meanings for the word fits the context?

_____

_____

chandeliers

Read the sentence that uses the word *chandeliers* and some of the sentences around it.

Look for context clues to the word's meaning. What clues showing **What the Word Is Used For** can you find?

_____

Think about the context clues and other information you already know.

_____

Predict a meaning for the word *chandelier*.

_____

Check your Word Wisdom Dictionary to be sure of the meaning of the word *chandelier*. Write the definition here.

_____

_____

🔓 Unlock the Meanings

Several words you studied in Part 1 have Latin roots. Knowing the meaning of these roots will help you unlock the meaning of many unfamiliar words. Each root is related to appearance.

Latin Root: **cand**
meaning: white
English word: *incandescent*
meaning: glowing with intense heat; very bright

Latin Root: **luc, lum, lus, lustr**
meaning: light, clear, brighten
English word: *luster*
meaning: gloss; sheen; brightness

Latin Root: **ple, pli**
meaning: fold
English word: *pliable*
meaning: easily bent or shaped; flexible

WORD LIST

luminary

ply

luminescent

chandelier

lucent

translucent

illustrious

supple

compliant

candid

Categorize by Roots Find these roots in the Word List. Write each word in the correct column. One word that comes from the *cand* root is spelled differently, and one word that comes from the *ple, pli* root is spelled differently. Then think of other words you know that come from the same Latin roots. Write each word in the correct column.

Latin Root:
cand

Latin Root:
luc, lum, lus, lustr

Latin Root:
ple, pli

_____

_____

_____

_____

_____

_____

_____

_____

_____

_____

_____

_____

_____

_____

_____

Appearance

Prefix	Meaning	Example
trans-	across, through, on the other side	**trans-** (through) + **luc** (light) + **-ent** (adj.) = **translucent**

Use Roots and Prefixes Circle any roots or prefixes that you find in the boldfaced words below. Use your knowledge of roots, prefixes, and context clues to write the meaning of each word. Check your definitions in the Word Wisdom Dictionary.

1 The GloFish™ is a **luminescent** creature that was genetically altered to give off light through chemical changes.

_____

2 Three of the bulbs in the **chandelier** needed to be replaced.

_____

3 Swimming and ballet help make the body **supple**.

_____

4 Carl Sandburg and Gwendolyn Brooks are **illustrious** poets from Illinois.

_____

5 That breed of cat is known for its calm, **compliant** personality.

_____

6 **Translucent** window shades let light in but provide privacy.

_____

7 Christopher Reeve, who played Superman, has become a **luminary** for people with spinal injuries.

_____

8 George has a **candid** way of saying what he honestly thinks.

_____

9 Warm winter sweaters are often made of three-**ply** woolen yarn.

_____

10 The sun is a **lucent** object in the sky.

_____

Process the Meanings

WORD LIST

luminary

ply

luminescent

chandelier

lucent

translucent

illustrious

supple

compliant

candid

Choose the Antonyms Write the word from the Word List that is an antonym for each word below.

Antonym	Vocabulary Word
1 misleading	_____
2 clumsy	_____
3 disagreeable	_____
4 unknown	_____

Choose the Correct Word Choose the vocabulary word in parentheses that correctly completes each sentence. Write the word on the line.

5 When the house was modernized, every _____ was replaced with track or recessed lighting fixtures. (chandelier, translucent)

6 At night, the _____ silver of the tiny fish made each wave dance as it approached the beach. (luminescent, illustrious)

7 From where we were sitting in the theater, we could see all the extra cast members on the other side of the _____ screen. (compliant, translucent)

8 "Fold the towel so that you have at least a double _____," explained the instructor from Be the Best Housekeeper. (candid, ply)

9 We expected to see dozens of movie stars when we visited Hollywood, California, but there wasn't a _____ in sight. (lucent, luminary)

10 The costumes sparkled with _____ comets, stars, and planets. (ply, lucent)

Connect the Words For each clue, choose the best word from the Word List. Use each word only once.

1 Sometimes it's best to be open and direct with people.

_____

2 People behind this kind of glass or fabric can be seen but not identified.

_____

3 This glows but does not give off much heat. _____

4 Many of today's paper products have more than one layer.

_____

5 Be careful not to bump your head on this decorative but practical item.

_____

6 This word could describe a dancer, an athlete, or a pair of fine leather boots.

_____

7 You might want an autograph from this particular person.

_____

8 This kind of person gets along particularly well in large groups.

_____

9 There is little doubt that a famous, successful person can also be described this way.

_____

10 This could describe a candle or a lamp in a window.

_____

Speak It! Describe an imaginary party for famous people that you would like to give. Tell about the people you would invite and why. Describe the setting, the food, and the entertainment. In your description, use as many words from the Word List in Part 2 as you can.

PART 3 Reference Skills

for Word Wisdom

A Movie Review:
Lost in Place

If you haven't seen the last movie in the Star World trilogy, don't bother. Although the first two movies in this series were awesome, *Poisoned Planet* can be described in one word: boring.

The movie opens in an **ornate** room with a **décor** that reminds me of an ancient sultan's palace. It definitely does not look like the headquarters of a space-age dictator from a faraway planet. The walls are draped with red velvet. Stone columns that are placed throughout the **cavernous** room are studded with sparkling jewels. The floor is covered with intricate patterns of tile.

The Dark Leader should be exhausted after all his battles in the first two movies. Instead, he looks energetic and **robust**. Previously, the Dark Leader had a sly and wicked expression that blended well with his sly and wicked activities. But, in this movie, he looks **placid** and content. His smile seems almost kind!

Gone are the fascinating little gnomes that used to bustle around the headquarters as they served the Dark Leader. In their place now are **nondescript** servants. In fact, the only **concrete** thing I can remember about them is that each one is starkly **monochromatic**: one is red, one is blue, one is green, and so on. Even their

skin and hair match their clothes. Other than that, they are entirely too ordinary for a Star World movie. They all have only two arms, two eyes, one head, and so on. As I said, this movie is boring!

Our hero Derk, on the other hand, is his usual **rustic** self. Wearing his cowboy hat and boots, he still looks as if he just left his ranch. I keep expecting him to ride in on his trusty horse. All his battles with the Dark Leader have done nothing to **disfigure** his handsome face.

What can I say about the plot of this movie? The Dark Leader has hatched another wicked plan to take over the universe. This time, he plans to envelop Planet Huradi in a poisonous gas. Breathing the gas will cause everyone to freeze in place, awaiting orders from the Dark Leader. Huradians will become his subjects—and build him more ornate palaces, I guess.

Of course, Derk risks his life to stop the Dark Leader's evil aggression, but he is captured and imprisoned before he can convince anyone of the danger. The other Huradians apparently did not watch the first two movies in this trilogy, as they seem totally unaware of the Dark Leader's wickedness. Still, Derk cleverly disguises himself and escapes from prison just in time to save Huradi, again.

If you have time to see this movie, do something else instead. Don't waste your time on *Poisoned Planet*!

Practice the Context Clues Strategy Here are two of the boldfaced words from the movie review on page 150. Use the context clues strategy you learned in Part 1 on page 139 to figure out the meanings of these words.

décor

📖 **Read** the sentence that uses the word *décor* and some of the sentences around it.

🔍 **Look** for context clues to the word's meaning. What clues showing **What the Word Is Used For** can you find?

_____

_____

💡 **Think** about the context clues and other information you already know.

_____

➡️ **Predict** a meaning for the word *décor*.

_____

✔️ **Check** your Word Wisdom Dictionary to be sure of the meaning of the word *décor*. Write the definition here.

_____

monochromatic

📖 **Read** the sentence that uses the word *monochromatic* and some of the sentences around it.

🔍 **Look** for context clues to the word's meaning. What clues showing **What the Word Is Used For** can you find?

_____

💡 **Think** about the context clues and other information you already know.

_____

➡️ **Predict** a meaning for the word *monochromatic*.

_____

✔️ **Check** your Word Wisdom Dictionary to be sure of the meaning of the word *monochromatic*. Write the definition here.

_____

Unlock the Meanings

Prefixes and Their Meanings A **prefix** is a word part that is put at the beginning of a word and changes the word's meaning. For example, you have already studied the prefix *re-*, which can mean "again," and the prefix *pre-*, which can mean "before." If you add the prefix *re-* to the verb *heat*, you get *reheat*, which means "to heat again." *Please reheat the soup because it's gotten cold.* If, however, you add the prefix *pre-* to the verb *heat*, you get *preheat*, which means "to heat before." *Be sure to preheat the oven before you put the cookies in to bake.*

Dictionaries often give the meaning of a prefix at the end of an entry. Complete dictionaries list prefixes and their meanings alphabetically. A prefix entry ends with a dash (–), which shows that the prefix is not a whole word. The abbreviation for prefix, *pref.*, also appears.

Figure Out the Meanings Find the prefix in each word below. When you write it, remember to end it with a dash. Look up the meaning of the prefix in a dictionary and write it below. Then list two other words you know with the same prefix.

Word	Prefix	Meaning of Prefix	Other Words With Prefix
1 monochromatic			
2 nondescript			
3 disfigure			
4 concrete			
5 incandescent			

Find the Meaning

1. Use context clues.
2. Look for a familiar root, prefix, or suffix.
3. If the context or a word part doesn't help, check the dictionary.

WORD LIST

ornate

décor

cavernous

robust

placid

nondescript

concrete

monochromatic

rustic

disfigure

Define the Words Follow the steps above to decide on the meaning of each boldfaced word. Write the meaning of the word. Then write 1, 2, or 3 to show which steps you used.

1 An **ornate** ring made of emeralds, sapphires, and rubies was on her finger.

_____

2 Terence couldn't think of a **concrete** example, so he lost the argument.

_____

3 For a small cat, Radullah certainly does have a **cavernous** yawn.

_____

4 Some people owe their **robust** long lives to clean air and a good diet.

_____

5 A blue shirt and a blue tie with a blue suit is a **monochromatic** look.

_____

6 Ruth was nervous about performing for the first time, but her solo was beautiful and her appearance was **placid**.

_____

7 The room's Victorian **décor** featured a floral carpet and a chandelier.

_____

8 Wearing a **nondescript** tan raincoat and beige hat, the undercover detective blended easily with all the similarly dressed commuters.

_____

9 Birdhouses and twig furniture added **rustic** touches to their tiny city patio.

_____

10 How did the storm **disfigure** that monument?

_____

WORD LIST

ornate

décor

cavernous

robust

placid

nondescript

concrete

monochromatic

rustic

disfigure

Choose the Correct Word Write the vocabulary word that best completes each sentence.

1 I can give you three _____ examples of what I mean; you will be impressed with the specific details.

2 Carrie called the _____ food that was served "mystery meat" because no one could identify it as beef or pork.

3 Neither one of my great grandparents is weak or fragile; in fact, the two of them are the most _____ people I know!

4 Do you like showy, _____ jewelry, or do you have simpler tastes?

5 With license plates on the walls and hats covering the ceiling, the restaurant had a most unusual _____.

6 Plant containers without saucers can be damaging; water can leak and _____ wooden floors and tabletops.

7 The cottage in the country had unfinished beds and tables that were delightfully rough and _____.

8 Deep Creek Lake is a calm, _____ spot where the fastest vehicle is a canoe, and more ducks swim than people.

9 The deserted house was _____; every room was huge!

10 Although the blanket had stripes of both purple and gray, it looked _____ because the light in the room was so dim.

Apply What You've Learned

Associate the Meanings Write the word from the Word List that best answers each question. You will need to change the ending of one word.

1 Which word describes a kind of example that is easy to understand because it is specific and detailed? _____

2 Which word do you associate with a space too large to have good acoustics?

_____

3 Early American chairs or Danish modern tables could be part of a room's what? _____

4 Which word describes a statue that is ruined?

_____

5 Which word describes someone who has never been sick a day in his or her life? _____

6 What kind of person could never be called "a bundle of nerves"?

_____

7 Which word would you associate with a hideaway in the country?

_____

8 If you like simple things without much decoration, which word describes objects that would not appeal to you? _____

9 Which word would describe an unrecognizable breed of dog?

_____

10 Which word means "of one color" or the opposite of *multicolored*?

_____

Write It! Describe your favorite room. You could focus your description on a room in your house, in a museum, or in another public building. Give specific details. Use as many words from the Word List in Part 3 as you can.

PART **4**

Review
for Word Wisdom

Categorize by Parts of Speech Sort the words in the Word List by part of speech. Write each word in the correct column. Some words belong in two columns. When you are finished, circle the words that have the roots *cand; luc, lum, lus,* and *lustr; ple* and *pli.*

WORD LIST

- kiln
- molten
- incandescent
- manipulate
- elongate
- pincers
- calipers
- pliable
- luster
- subtle
- luminary
- ply
- luminescent
- chandelier
- lucent
- translucent
- illustrious
- supple
- compliant
- candid
- ornate
- décor
- cavernous
- robust
- placid
- nondescript
- concrete
- monochromatic
- rustic
- disfigure

Nouns	Verbs	Adjectives

Answer the Questions Use what you have learned about the vocabulary words to answer each question. Underline the correct answers.

1 Which word names something hanging over a dining room table?

       luminary   chandelier

2 Which word describes a quiet, peaceful person or place?

       placid   robust

3 What kind of cabins would you expect at a hunting and fishing camp?

       ornate   rustic

4 Which word could describe sights like high ceilings or hollow spaces?

       luminescent   cavernous

5 Which word describes what happens when a metal is heated and liquefied?

       molten   compliant

6 Which word names the result of using silver polish and a soft cloth on a dirty piece of jewelry?

       ply   luster

7 Which word applies to someone giving a confession?

       candid   pliable

8 Which word is the antonym of the words *dull* and *gloomy*?

       lucent   monochromatic

9 Which word would you apply to something that glows in the dark?

       incandescent   illustrious

10 Which word names someone who might speak at the opening of a museum?

       décor   luminary

Taking Vocabulary Tests

TEST-TAKING STRATEGY

An analogy test gives you a pair of words. Your task is to identify another pair of words that have the same relationship as the given pair. The given pair may be synonyms, antonyms, part and whole, object and action, and object and purpose. Say a sentence to yourself that expresses the relationship between the given words. Then eliminate answer choices that express different relationships.

Sample:

scale : weigh :: ___ : ___ (A scale weighs. The relationship is an object and its purpose.)

○ ply : fold (The words are synonyms. A ply does not fold.)

○ luminary : smiles (A luminary is not an object. His or her purpose is not to smile.)

○ chandelier : ornate (*Ornate* may describe a chandelier, but it is not its purpose.)

● kiln : dry (This pair shows the same relationship as the given pair—an object and its purpose.)

Practice Test Fill in the circle of the word pair that best expresses the same relationship as the given pair. The symbol : stands for "is to." The symbol :: stands for "as."

1 shrink : decrease ::
- ○ disfigure : damage
- ○ manipulate : hands
- ○ measure : calipers
- ○ elongate : time

2 nozzle : spout ::
- ○ ply : cashmere
- ○ distance : calipers
- ○ pincers : tweezers
- ○ kiln : pottery

3 vacant : occupied ::
- ○ supple : bend
- ○ concrete : real
- ○ illustrious : famous
- ○ nondescript : vivid

4 noisy : crowd ::
- ○ compliant : law
- ○ translucent : lens
- ○ supple : rock
- ○ robust : healthy

5 mud : syrupy ::
- ○ illustrious : star
- ○ monochromatic : color
- ○ moon : luminescent
- ○ ply : verbal

6 jolly : happy ::
- ○ easy : difficult
- ○ fancy : ornate
- ○ supple : pillow
- ○ concrete : sidewalk

7 small : enormous ::
- ○ tasty : snack
- ○ boss : work
- ○ hammer : nail
- ○ candid : secretive

8 dog : bark ::
- ○ chandelier : shine
- ○ robust : tiny
- ○ desk : table
- ○ cave : lucent

9 soft : supple ::
- ○ read : book
- ○ rough : rustic
- ○ décor : ornate
- ○ sun : shine

10 dig : shovel ::
- ○ pool : swim
- ○ couch : sit
- ○ placid : molten
- ○ measure : calipers

Build New Words

Borrowed Words The richness of our language is partly a result of contacts with other cultures. From them we have borrowed ideas and objects, along with their names. Some experts think that almost every language in the world has contributed something to English.

Two of the words in this unit, *décor* and *chandelier*, come from the French language. The word *décor* has kept its original French accent mark. The word *chandelier* has kept its French spelling but is pronounced differently in English. Read these words that come to English from French:

blasé	entrée	naïve
bureau	esprit de corps	nonchalant
café	etiquette	potpourri
cliché	faux pas	rendezvous
clarinet	fiancé	resumé

Investigate Words From French Choose five of the French words above to look up in a dictionary. Practice the pronunciation of the word and read its definition. Then write a sentence in which you illustrate your understanding of how the word can be used.

1 _____

2 _____

3 _____

4 _____

5 _____

Speak It! Deliver a speech in which you describe someone or something. Use as many words from the Word List in Part 4 as you can. Try to use some French words or phrases, too!

Context Clues

for Word Wisdom

Time for Change:
Cell Phones Have Changed Our Lives

New inventions often impact how we live. New technology has influenced the way we communicate, entertain ourselves, and travel. Read how one product—the cell phone—has changed some of our behavior patterns.

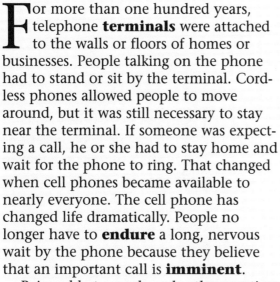

For more than one hundred years, telephone **terminals** were attached to the walls or floors of homes or businesses. People talking on the phone had to stand or sit by the terminal. Cordless phones allowed people to move around, but it was still necessary to stay near the terminal. If someone was expecting a call, he or she had to stay home and wait for the phone to ring. That changed when cell phones became available to nearly everyone. The cell phone has changed life dramatically. People no longer have to **endure** a long, nervous wait by the phone because they believe that an important call is **imminent**.

Being able to reach each other anytime and anywhere has definitely changed our **orientation** to the world around us. Spouses can let each other know right away when they are stuck in traffic or running an errand after work. Also, if drivers get **stranded** because their cars break down, their **ceaseless** wait for assistance is over. Now they can use a cell phone and know that help is coming soon. In the **interim,** they can call home to explain the delay, order some take-out food, or chat with friends.

The benefits of cell phones are enormous. They help people **sustain** their busy schedules. They are important for people in emergency situations. However, researchers have concluded that the cell phone is the **precursor** of some bad habits that people didn't have before. Cell phones have created what experts call "soft time." In other words, to some people, being on time doesn't matter as much as it used to.

Because people can always be in touch with each other, plans and schedules have become more **transitory**. If you can't meet at 5:00 P.M., you can call and say that you'll be there at 5:30 P.M.

The ability to receive a phone call anywhere we are has not only enabled us to communicate more freely, but it has also impacted negatively on those around us. People in movie theaters and restaurants are now often forced to listen to the cell-phone conversations of others.

While improving our lives in so many ways, cell phones also may have made us less polite and less responsible people.

Time

UNIT
8

Context Clues Strategy

Look for the Location or Setting

EXAMPLE: Not wanting to disturb the peace and protection that the *sanctuary* of the museum provided, Carla shut off her cell phone.

CLUE: The words *peace and protection* and *of the museum* describe the setting for *sanctuary*. A *sanctuary* must be a place that offers peace and protection.

Here is another strategy for using context clues. Use it to figure out the meaning of the word *terminals* from the essay on page 160.

Read the sentence with the unknown word and some of the sentences around it.

For more than one hundred years, telephone **terminals** *were attached to the walls or floors of homes or businesses.*

Look for context clues. What clues showing the **Location or Setting** can you find?

The article says *telephone terminals were attached to walls or floors of homes or businesses.* Those words give a location for the word *terminals.*

Think about the context clues and other helpful information you already know.

At home, we have a phone that is attached to the wall by a cord at one end. I know that cell phones are not attached to anything.

Predict a meaning for the word.

Terminal must mean "something attached at the end."

Check your Word Wisdom Dictionary to be sure of the meaning. Decide which of the meanings for the word fits the context.

A *terminal* is "a mechanical or electrical device in which some type of connection is established."

Unlock the Meanings

Practice the Strategy   Here are two of the boldfaced words from the essay on page 160. Use the context clues strategy on page 161 to figure out the meaning of each word.

orientation

Read the sentence that uses the word *orientation* and some of the sentences around it.

Look for context clues. What clues showing the **Location or Setting** can you find?

_____

Think about the context clues. What other helpful information do you know?

_____

Predict a meaning for the word *orientation*.

_____

Check your Word Wisdom Dictionary to see how it defines the word *orientation*. Which of the meanings for the word fits the context?

_____

precursor

Read the sentence that uses the word *precursor* and some of the sentences around it.

Look for context clues. What clues showing the **Location or Setting** can you find?

_____

Think about the context clues. What other information do you know?

_____

Predict a meaning for the word *precursor*.

_____

Check a dictionary to be sure of the meaning of the word *precursor*. Write the dictionary definition.

_____

Use Context Clues You have been introduced to three words from the essay on page 160. These words are checked off in the Word List. In the first column, write the other seven words from the Word List. In the second column, predict a meaning for each word. Then look up the meaning of the word in your Word Wisdom Dictionary. In the third column, write the dictionary meaning that fits the context.

Vocabulary Word	Your Prediction	Dictionary Says
1		
2		
3		
4		
5		
6		
7		

Process the Meanings

WORD LIST

terminal

endure

imminent

orientation

strand

ceaseless

interim

sustain

precursor

transitory

Identify Synonyms or Antonyms Decide on a synonym or an antonym (as indicated in parentheses) for each boldfaced word from the Word List. Write your choice on the blank line.

1 transitory (synonym) _____

    a. brief   b. permanent   c. confusing   d. silly

2 interim (synonym) _____

    a. time   b. long   c. brief   d. deep
      period   vacation   amazement   crevice

3 terminal (synonym) _____

    a. phone   b. pole   c. ending   d. control box

4 sustain (synonym) _____

    a. harden   b. depart   c. refuse   d. maintain

5 endure (antonym) _____

    a. promise to   b. refuse to   c. to stop   d. decide to
      arrive   leave   sleep

6 imminent (synonym) _____

    a. afraid   b. exhausted   c. unusual   d. upcoming

7 ceaseless (antonym) _____

    a. artificial   b. leisurely   c. short   d. embarrassed

8 strand (antonym) _____

    a. stay with   b. leave behind   c. explain away   d. take off

9 orientation (synonym) _____

    a. planet   b. confusion   c. humor   d. bearings

10 precursor (synonym) _____

    a. aftereffect   b. forerunner   c. first-class   d. second-prize
                                        athlete   winner

Apply What You've Learned

Use the Words Correctly Complete the sentences by choosing the phrase that best explains or illustrates the boldfaced vocabulary word. Write the letter of your choice on the blank line.

_____ **1** Someone who thinks of life as **transitory** would say that we
   a. are here today and gone tomorrow.
   b. all follow a different drummer.

_____ **2** If someone **strands** you at a party, you
   a. probably won't be happy with that person for a while.
   b. most likely will want to celebrate with that person immediately.

_____ **3** The **precursor** of an invention is
   a. a new idea that comes from the invention.
   b. something that led up to the invention.

_____ **4** A **ceaseless** storm
   a. may seem to go on forever.
   b. is over before you know it.

_____ **5** If you have to **endure** hard work to buy shoes,
   a. you may appreciate the shoes even more.
   b. you might believe that good things are easy to get.

_____ **6** If a blizzard is **imminent**, it would be wise to
   a. put away boots and shovels until next year.
   b. stock up on food, water, and radio batteries.

_____ **7** To find your **orientation** at a new mall,
   a. look at the map of the mall to see where everything is.
   b. walk around until you get tired.

_____ **8** A runner who cannot **sustain** the group's pace
   a. outruns most of his or her teammates.
   b. will probably fall behind.

_____ **9** The **interim** between an afternoon play and an evening play probably
   a. lasts several hours.
   b. means that people don't like the show.

_____ **10** When the bus arrives at the bus **terminal**,
   a. passengers have to get off the bus.
   b. school ends for summer vacation.

Write It! Write an article for a newspaper column called "From Time to Time." Choose one of these ideas for your topic: Ahead of Its (or His/Her) Time, At One Time, Time Flies, or Pass the Time of Day. Use as many vocabulary words from Part 1 as you can.

PART 2

Latin Roots

for Word Wisdom

Endless Time:
Dreamtime in Australia

What does *time* mean to you? *Time* has a different meaning for people whose culture is 40,000 to 60,000 years old. People have lived in Australia for all of those centuries. They have passed down their many customs and traditions from ancient times to today.

The **original** people who lived in Australia are called Aborigines. Groups of Aborigines still live there. Since ancient times, the Aborigines have used Dreamtime to explain the **origin** of their homeland. For **aboriginal** people, Dreamtime is a beginning that has never ended. Dreamtime includes the past, the **current** time, and the future.

Each group of Aborigines has its own collection of Dreamtime stories. However, one basic theme is **recurrent** in most of them. According to most of these stories, Earth was empty before Dreamtime began. Then spirits came down to Earth. Some of the spirits were in human form. They created men and women and plants and animals. These spirits set laws for people to follow in all aspects of their lives. For example, they declared how food would be shared. They **predetermined** how the Aborigines would marry and how they would bury their dead.

Then, according to some Dreamtime stories, the spirits vanished from sight. They went to live in secret places. They still live there today but are hidden from view. Some live in trees and water holes, while others live in the sky. Some of the spirits became natural forces, such as rain, wind, and lightning. Others became stars or hills. Some spirits still live on Earth, so Dreamtime has not been **terminated**.

The Aborigines have survived amazing changes. About 30,000 years ago, Australia was green and fertile, with lakes and giant animals. However, about 20,000 years ago, the Ice Age occurred. Temperatures dropped, and plants died. Cold, dry winds roared across the land. They created huge sand dunes. The Aborigines had trouble finding food and water. Perhaps four out of every five people died. The most **durable** of them managed to survive. They located small patches of forest where they found food and water.

The **duration** of the Ice Age was 5,000 to 6,000 years. Then temperatures started to rise. By 10,000 years ago, the climate of Australia was much like it is now. During all of this time, the Aborigines coped and survived. They continued to tell their stories about Dreamtime to their children and their children's children.

During these centuries, Aboriginal groups were spread across the continent. Some traded often with other groups, but others were isolated. For them, contact with other groups was a very rare **occurrence**. Thus, groups developed in different ways. By the time Europeans landed on Australian shores in 1606, the Aboriginal groups spoke 250 different languages.

When you think about time, remember the people of Australia. They continue to experience time in the fullest sense: yesterday, today, and tomorrow.

Practice the Context Clues Strategy Here are two of the boldfaced words from the essay on page 166. Use the context clues strategy you learned in Part 1 on page 161 to figure out the meanings of these words.

predetermined

Read the sentence that uses the word *predetermined* and some of the sentences around it.

Look for context clues. What clues showing the **Location or Setting** can you find?

_____

Think about the context clues. What other helpful information do you know?

_____

Predict a meaning for the word *predetermine*.

_____

Check your Word Wisdom Dictionary to be sure of the meaning of the word *predetermine*. Which of the meanings for the word fits the context?

_____

durable

Read the sentence that uses the word *durable* and some of the sentences around it.

Look for context clues. What clues showing the **Location or Setting** can you find?

_____

Think about the context clues. What other helpful information do you know?

_____

Predict a meaning for the word *durable*.

_____

Check your Word Wisdom Dictionary to be sure of the meaning of the word *durable*. Write the definition here.

_____

🔒 Unlock the Meanings

Several words you studied in Part 1 have Latin roots. Knowing the meaning of these roots will help you unlock the meaning of many unfamiliar words. Each root is related to time.

Latin Root: **ori**

meaning: to begin

English word: *orientation*

meaning: where you are in relation to your surroundings

Latin Root: **cour, cur**

meaning: to run

English word: *precursor*

meaning: something that comes before

Latin Root: **dur**

meaning: lasting, hard

English word: *endure*

meaning: to continue through hardship

Latin Root: **term, termin**

meaning: limit

English word: *terminal*

meaning: something at the end

WORD LIST

original

origin

aboriginal

current

recurrent

predetermine

terminate

durable

duration

occurrence

Categorize by Roots Find these roots in the Word List. Write each word below the correct root. Then think of other words you know that come from the same Latin roots. Write each word in the correct place.

Latin Root: **ori**

_____

_____

_____

_____

Latin Root: **term, termin**

_____

_____

_____

Time

Latin Root: **cour, cur**

_____

_____

_____

Latin Root: **dur**

_____

_____

_____

Prefix	Meaning	Example
ab-	from	ab- (from) + ori (begin) + gin + -al (adj.) = aboriginal

Use Roots and Prefixes Circle the root and any prefix you find in the boldfaced words. Then, use context clues, roots, and prefixes to write the meaning of each word. Check your definitions in a dictionary.

1 This is a poster of a famous painting; the **original** is in a museum.

_____

2 The number of tables set for the reception is **predetermined** by the number of guests.

_____

3 Denim is a **durable** fabric, so clothes made from it should last for years.

_____

4 The **recurrent** chorus, sung six times, is more famous than the song itself.

_____

5 **Aboriginal** art is unique, with its geometric forms and rich colors.

_____

6 What is the most **current** research on teaching reading?

_____

7 The **duration** of the storm was short; the sun reappeared in minutes.

_____

8 If you **terminate** the contract within five days, your money will be refunded.

_____

9 The **origins** of many rivers can be found high in the mountains.

_____

10 Seeing famous people in our neighborhood is not a typical **occurrence**.

_____

Process the Meanings

Replace the Underlined Words Write the best word from the Word List to take the place of the underlined word or words in each sentence.

1 We can <u>decide in advance</u> the outcome of the game.

_____

2 The Ainu were among the <u>earliest known</u> people of Japan.

_____

3 Seeing deer at dusk is an everyday <u>happening</u> in a rustic setting.

_____

4 Please <u>end</u> your phone call now because we need to leave soon.

_____

5 What are your plans for the <u>length of time</u> of your stay in New York?

_____

Choose the Antonyms   Write the word from the Word List that is the best antonym for each word or phrase.

6 copy _____

7 fragile _____

8 end point _____

9 not happening regularly_____

10 out-of-date _____

Choose the Synonyms Write the word from the Word List that is a synonym for each word.

11 dismiss _____

12 event _____

13 continuation _____

14 premeditate _____

15 native _____

Apply What You've Learned

Complete the Sentences Use what you've learned about the boldfaced words to write an ending for each sentence.

1 One quality that makes a friendship **durable** is _____

_____

2 An unexpected **occurrence** was _____

_____

3 A **current** topic or issue in the news is _____

_____

4 For the **duration** of our next summer vacation, I _____

_____

5 An outcome that is **predetermined** is _____

_____

Demonstrate Word Knowledge Answer each question by writing **yes** or **no** on the line. Be prepared to discuss the reason for your choice.

_____ **6** Would someone **terminate** the search for a book after finding it?

_____ **7** Does the **origin** of a rumor depend on whether the rumor is true or false?

_____ **8** Would you expect **aboriginal** wildlife to replace a housing development?

_____ **9** If you have an **original** approach to solving a problem, is your idea fresh and new?

_____ **10** Does a **recurrent** nightmare happen only once?

Speak It! Pretend that you are in charge of a big project in your school, such as the production of a play, the publication of a computer magazine, or something else. Tell about your plans and your time frame. Use as many vocabulary words from Part 2 as you can.

PART 3 Reference Skills

Passing the Time:
Time Management

Time management is not just for adults. Young people must organize their time wisely, too. Good time management allows you to take care of your responsibilities, reduce stress, and have time left over for some fun.

To manage your time well, begin by setting goals at the beginning of the school year. As an **annual** activity, you might set a goal for each of your classes. You could challenge yourself to raise your usual grade in at least one of your classes. First, decide what grade you will work toward. Then, figure out how much time you'll need to spend working toward that grade.

As part of your plan for the year, you might tentatively decide which sports and other activities will be part of your regular schedule. If possible, find out when practices and meetings are planned so you know which activities overlap or even **coincide**. If volleyball practice always starts at the same time that the Ecology Club meets, for example, you might have to decide which one is more important to you. If the overlaps are just **occasional**, perhaps you can participate in both activities. Still, do not make any rash or **premature** decisions before you are certain of the scheduling.

One of the most **persistent** questions for students is this: "How can I make the most of my study time?" Naturally, you want the hours you study to be the most productive possible. To study wisely, first determine what period of the day is the best study time for you. Are you a morning person or a night person? When is it easiest for you to focus? After answering this question, plan your study time accordingly and **postpone** your errands for times when your brain is tired.

Now that you have identified a study time, tackle your difficult subjects first, when you are fresh. Also, focus on those subject areas in which you want to raise your grades. Study in time blocks of twenty minutes or so with short breaks in between. That way, you can concentrate for a while and **anticipate** the break you have planned. Even while you are taking your break, your brain will still be thinking about the topic you are studying. **Continuous** studying, on the other hand, will soon tire you and eventually will encourage you to waste time. You may actually spend longer with your books but benefit less.

When you have an **impending** test, set up a special study plan. Set aside an extra hour, for example, on the four **consecutive** days before the test. If you study during those times, you will not need to cram the night before the test and miss sleep. Being tired might affect your performance on a test as much as not studying. Also, when you cram for a test, you are less likely to retain the information.

Keeping track of how you actually spend your time for one week might surprise you. You may discover some time-wasters that you can easily eliminate. Learning how to manage your time wisely will help you for the rest of your life.

Practice the Context Clues Strategy Here are two of the boldfaced words from the essay on page 172. Use the context clues strategy you learned in Part 1 on page 161 to figure out the meanings of these words.

coincide

Read the sentence that uses the word *coincide* and some of the sentences around it.

Look for context clues. What clues showing the **Location or Setting** can you find?

_____

Think about the context clues. What other helpful information do you know?

_____

Predict a meaning for the word *coincide*.

_____

Check your Word Wisdom Dictionary to be sure of the meaning of the word *coincide*. Which of the meanings for the word fits the context?

_____

consecutive

Read the sentence that uses the word *consecutive* and some of the sentences around it.

Look for context clues to the word's meaning. What clues showing the **Location or Setting** can you find?

_____

Think about the context clues. What other helpful information do you know?

_____

Predict a meaning for the word *consecutive*.

_____

Check your Word Wisdom Dictionary to be sure of the meaning of the word *consecutive*. Write the definition here.

_____

Unlock the Meanings

Use Part-of-Speech Labels Use the context to determine the part of speech of the word *annual* in each sentence below. Write the part of speech and the correct definition on the blank line.

1 Dina had several poems published in the school's literary **annual**.

_____

2 The **annual** activity fee at the community center is twenty-five dollars.

_____

3 The Thanksgiving Parade on Main Street is an **annual** event.

_____

4 **Annuals** such as impatiens and petunias provide color in our summer garden.

_____

5 My family has an **annual** tradition of a picnic in honor of our grandparents.

_____

Find the Meaning

1. Use context clues.
2. Look for a familiar root, prefix, or suffix.
3. If the context or a word part doesn't help, check the dictionary.

WORD LIST

annual

coincide

occasional

premature

persistent

postpone

anticipate

continuous

impending

consecutive

Define the Words Follow the steps above to write the meaning of each boldfaced word. Write 1, 2, or 3 to show which steps you used.

1 Experienced dance partners know how to **anticipate** each other's moves.

_____

2 Sarah grew to love modern art during her **occasional** trips to the museum.

_____

3 Because of the storm, we had to **postpone** our departure by several days.

_____

4 The **persistent** ringing of the phone during dinner was hard to ignore.

_____

5 When we answered the phone, it was Joe, worrying about an **impending** problem at school.

_____

6 My birthday party always **coincides** with the Fourth-of-July celebration.

_____

7 It is **premature** to predict the team's status before the season starts.

_____

8 The Gardinis' **annual** family reunion takes place every October.

_____

9 Students who are absent for three **consecutive** days need a doctor's note when they return to school.

_____

10 The **continuous** line of the horizon seemed to stretch forever.

_____

Process the Meanings

WORD LIST

- annual
- coincide
- occasional
- premature
- persistent
- postpone
- anticipate
- continuous
- impending
- consecutive

Choose the Correct Word Write the word from the Word List that best completes each sentence. Use each word only once. You will need to change the ending of some words.

1 So many musicians had the flu that the performance was _____ until the following week.

2 The letters *q, r, s, t, u, v* are six _____ letters of the alphabet.

3 Residents of the coastal town _____ the force of the hurricane by boarding up their windows.

4 The newscaster made a _____ announcement about the election before the polls closed.

5 Knocking at the door again and again, George was _____ in trying to be heard above the noise inside.

6 This year, the first day of our summer vacation and Memorial Day _____.

7 The _____ hum of crickets drowned out the noise from the highway.

8 This year's _____ fund-raising carnival was the most successful in four years.

9 Mom's _____ headaches don't happen often, but she wants to have her eyes checked.

10 Grandpa's _____ retirement seemed far away before, but now it seems just around the corner.

Apply What You've Learned

Give Examples Write a sentence that gives an example of each of the following. Use the boldfaced vocabulary word in your answer.

1 an **occasional** activity you would like to do more often

_____

2 an event that had to be **postponed**

_____

3 an **annual** tradition you have or would like to start

_____

4 something that goes in **consecutive** order

_____

5 two things that **coincide** (or once **coincided**) in your life

_____

Complete the Sentences Complete each sentence.

6 No one could have **anticipated** _____

_____

7 Carly was **persistent** in her attempts to _____

_____

8 The weather forecast was **premature** because _____

_____

9 During the movie, the **continuous** _____

_____

10 One sign of an **impending** storm is _____

_____

Write It! Write about a situation you recall in which time played an important role. For example, you might have had only ten minutes to get to practice one day, or you needed more time to write a report. Use as many vocabulary words from Part 3 as you can.

Review

for Word Wisdom

WORD LIST

- terminal
- endure
- imminent
- orientation
- strand
- ceaseless
- interim
- sustain
- precursor
- transitory
- original
- origin
- aboriginal
- current
- recurrent
- predetermine
- terminate
- durable
- duration
- occurrence
- annual
- coincide
- occasional
- premature
- persistent
- postpone
- anticipate
- continuous
- impending
- consecutive

Categorize by Syllables Say each word to yourself. Count the syllables. Write the word in the correct column. Check off the words on the list as you work. When you are finished, circle every word that has the root *ori, cour, cur, dur, term,* or *termin.*

Words having one syllable

_____
_____
_____
_____
_____
_____

Words having two syllables

_____
_____
_____
_____
_____
_____

Words having three syllables

_____
_____
_____
_____
_____
_____
_____
_____
_____
_____
_____
_____

Words having four syllables

_____
_____
_____
_____
_____
_____

Words having five syllables

_____
_____
_____
_____
_____
_____

Answer the Questions Choose the best vocabulary word in the box to answer each question.

occurrence	annual	original	terminate	consecutive
endure	ceaseless	transitory	orientation	occasional
persistent	postpone	duration	origin	durable

_____ **1** Which verb means "to end"?

_____ **2** Which adjective goes best with *magazine subscription* and *salary*?

_____ **3** Which adjective describes the length of time spent waiting for a late bus?

_____ **4** Which noun names a situation or event?

_____ **5** Which adjective describes events that take place from time to time?

_____ **6** Which noun names the process of deciding where you are?

_____ **7** Which adjective describes the five games in a row that your favorite team wins?

_____ **8** Which adjective describes something that does not last?

_____ **9** Which verb tells how someone stays alive in the Arctic?

_____ **10** Which adjective describes something that no one has ever thought of?

_____ **11** Which noun refers to a period of time?

_____ **12** Which adjective describes someone who won't give up?

_____ **13** Which noun is a synonym for *beginning*?

_____ **14** Which verb is a synonym for *delay*?

_____ **15** Which adjective is an antonym of *flimsy*?

Taking Vocabulary Tests

TEST-TAKING STRATEGY

Sentence-completion questions test your ability to choose the correct word for the context. First, read the entire sentence. Think about its structure and meaning. Then read all of the answer choices. Eliminate as many obviously wrong ones as you can. When you find an answer you think is correct, insert the word in the blank. Read the sentence again to make sure that it makes sense.

Sample:

Carpeting in public places has to be ___ enough to withstand the effects of bad weather and many feet.

Ⓐ occasional *(Carpeting from time to time makes no sense.)*

Ⓑ annual *(Yearly carpeting doesn't make sense either.)*

Ⓒ ceaseless *(Never-ending carpeting doesn't make sense.)*

Ⓓ durable *(This is the correct and logical choice. Carpeting has to be tough and lasting.)*

Practice Test Fill in the circle of the item that best completes each sentence.

1 It can be hard to ___ a conversation with someone who gives only *yes* and *no* answers to your questions.
Ⓐ sustain
Ⓑ terminate
Ⓒ predetermine
Ⓓ postpone

2 In the winter, Claire was awakened repeatedly by the ___ scratch of lilac branches against her window.
Ⓐ aboriginal
Ⓑ consecutive
Ⓒ current
Ⓓ persistent

3 Because John knew the ___ of the misunderstanding, he was able to go to the right person to get it corrected.
Ⓐ duration
Ⓑ origin
Ⓒ interim
Ⓓ occurrence

4 According to the most ___ report, food prices have gone down this month.
Ⓐ current
Ⓑ terminal
Ⓒ ceaseless
Ⓓ original

5 When the electricity went out in the preschool, the children did not lose their ___ but confidently filed out of the unlit building in orderly lines.
Ⓐ precursor
Ⓑ occurrence
Ⓒ interim
Ⓓ orientation

Play with Language

You know that an **idiom** is a phrase or expression with a special meaning. An idiom dictionary explains the meaning of idioms. If you look up the word *time*, for example, you will find such idioms as "against time," "high time," and "time on (one's) hands." "High time," for example, does not mean that time is somehow high in the sky. The expression is an idiom that means it's time to do something—for instance, "It's high time that we start packing for the trip."

Match Words and Idioms Choose a vocabulary word from the box to match each group of idioms. Use each vocabulary word only once.

> current   impending   recurrent
> postpone   endure   terminate

I drag your feet
hold your breath
put in a holding pattern

_____

2 in the cards
looming large
on the horizon

_____

3 hold out
brave a thousand years
put up with

_____

4 going over the same ground
singing the same old song
time and again

_____

5 brand new
up-to-date
just out

_____

6 nip it in the bud
cut it out
hit the brakes

_____

Speak It! Think about your life two years ago and your life now. How have the times changed? What is different about you? Tell about the contrast between the two time periods. Use as many vocabulary words from this Time unit as you can.

PART 1

Context Clues

for Word Wisdom

Both Sides of the Story:
The Common Squirrel

Whether you live in the city or the country, you've probably seen gray squirrels. They romp through the trees and scamper across rooftops. They work as hard as they play. How you feel about these creatures is based on whether your experiences with them have been positive or negative.

A nimal lovers are the squirrel's **staunch** supporters, like loyal and steady sports fans. While many people consider squirrels pests, animal lovers really like and care about them.

Half body and half tail, the squirrel is an amazing climber and leaper. With powerful hind legs and sharp claws, it can run headfirst down a tree trunk or across miles of telephone wires. Its bushy tail serves as a balancing pole or a parachute. Even anti-squirrel people have to respect a squirrel's athletic ability and feel **grudging** admiration.

Bird feeders are where squirrels cross the line for many people. Feeding birds is a popular hobby in the United States. Squirrels can ruin that hobby. Squirrels' brains may be the size of a walnut, but squirrels are intelligent. It doesn't take long for a squirrel to figure out how to get into any bird feeder. Even feeders designed to be squirrel-proof can't stop it. The squirrel has an **obsession** with seeds and nuts, just like a bee's fascination with flowers. Notorious thieves, they help themselves to large amounts of food meant for birds. As **pesky** as flies, they can take over the feeders by frightening off most of the birds.

Homeowners might agree to a **truce** with squirrels if the squirrels stopped at bird feeders. Given any chance, though, squirrels will build their nests in attics and garages. They can **deface** roofs and railings. Their jaws and front teeth allow them to chew through anything—plastic, wood, or metal. Adventurous squirrels climb down fireplace chimneys. They can fit into anything they can get their head through. They cost homeowners expensive repairs and endless **grief**.

Like the prejudice some people have against snakes, many people have a **bias** against squirrels. However, the small **faction** of squirrel defenders appreciates the squirrel as a force of nature and a source of entertainment. If you are feeling unhappy, or **despondent,** you might try watching these energetic acrobats. Squirrels can cheer you up—and the entertainment is free!

Context Clues Strategy

Look for What the Word Is Compared With

EXAMPLE: Like her uncle, who delays doing any task, Caroline is a *procrastinator*.

CLUE: The words *like her uncle, who delays doing any task* compare the word *procrastinator* with something familiar. The word *like* signals a clue. You can conclude that *procrastinator* means "someone who delays doing things."

Here are the steps for using this context clues strategy to figure out the meaning of the word *obsession*, which appeared in the essay you just read.

Read the sentence with the unknown word and some of the sentences around it.

The squirrel has an **obsession** *with seeds and nuts, just like a bee's fascination with flowers.*

Look for context clues. What clues showing **What the Word Is Compared With** can you find?

Obsession is compared with the word *fascination*.

Think about the context clues and other helpful information you already know.

I know that some people have an obsession with things like new clothes or chocolate. They think about these things often.

Predict a meaning for the word.

Obsession must mean "an idea that is thought of over and over."

Check your Word Wisdom Dictionary to be sure of the meaning.

The word *obsession* means "an idea or desire that keeps coming into the mind."

Unlock the Meanings

Practice the Strategy Here are two of the boldfaced words from the essay on page 182. Use the context clues strategy on page 183 to figure out the meaning of each word.

staunch

Read the sentence that uses the word *staunch* and some of the sentences around it.

Look for context clues. What clues showing **What the Word Is Compared With** can you find?

_____

Think about the context clues. What other helpful information do you know?

_____

Predict a meaning for the word *staunch*.

_____

Check the Word Wisdom Dictionary to see how it defines the word *staunch*. Write the definition here.

_____

bias

Read the sentence that uses the word *bias* and some of the sentences around it.

Look for context clues. What clues showing **What the Word Is Compared With** can you find?

_____

Think about the context clues. What other helpful information do you know?

_____

Predict a meaning for the word *bias*.

_____

Check a dictionary to see how it defines the word *bias*. Decide which of the meanings in the dictionary fits the context.

_____

WORD LIST

✔ staunch
grudging
✔ obsession
pesky
truce
deface
grief
✔ bias
faction
despondent

Use Context Clues   You have been introduced to three of the words from the essay on page 182. These words have been checked off in the Word List. In the first column, write the other seven words from the Word List. In the second column, predict a meaning for each word using context clues. Then look up the meaning of the word in the Word Wisdom Dictionary. In the third column, write the dictionary meaning that fits the context.

	Vocabulary Word	Your Prediction	Dictionary Says
1			
2			
3			
4			
5			
6			
7			

Process the Meanings

WORD LIST

staunch

grudging

obsession

pesky

truce

deface

grief

bias

faction

despondent

Replace the Words   Write the word from the Word List that best replaces the underlined word or phrase. You will need to add an ending to one word.

1 Because of the <u>troublesome</u> bugs, Harry screened in the front porch.

_____

2 The <u>small group in the larger group</u> disagrees with the leader.

_____

3 People <u>spoil the look</u> of trees by carving initials in the bark.

_____

4 With <u>unwilling</u> acceptance that the concert was sold out, we went home.

_____

5 Many people are <u>faithful and dependable</u> supporters of equal rights.

_____

6 Don't let this rainy day make you <u>unhappy</u>!

_____

7 Everyone should avoid <u>prejudices</u> against people and groups.

_____

8 Carla's <u>idea that dominated her thoughts</u> with cleaning kept her from enjoying her free time.

_____

9 Many people feel <u>deep suffering</u> at the loss of a beloved pet.

_____

10 By staying at opposite ends of the room, the cat and the dog reached a <u>temporary suspension of hostilities</u>.

_____

Demonstrate Word Knowledge Use what you've learned about the boldfaced words to answer the questions or follow the directions.

1 What could be done about a fence that has been **defaced**? _____

_____

2 Describe something in your life that is **pesky**. _____

_____

3 Why does a **bias** for or against something not make sense? _____

_____

4 Give an example of an **obsession** that people might have. _____

_____

5 What can help if you feel **despondent**? _____

_____

6 What (or whom) are you a **staunch** supporter of? _____

_____

7 What is something that might cause a person **grief**? _____

_____

8 What would you expect from someone with a **grudging** attitude? _____

_____

9 Why is a **truce** not as good as a permanent solution? _____

_____

10 If most people were in favor of a new bus station, what opinion might a **faction** have?

_____

Write It! Write about a disagreement you once had with someone. Try to tell both sides of the story. How was the disagreement resolved? Use as many words from the Word List in Part 1 as you can.

PART 2 Latin Roots

for Word Wisdom

Pros and Cons:
School Dress Codes

Does your school have a dress code? Does it regulate what you wear to classes every day? If your school has no code, should it adopt one? Is a school dress code a good idea—or a mistake?

Some people think a dress code is **beneficial** because it eliminates the need for students to keep up with the latest fads. If everyone wears the same uniform, no one will be under pressure to buy a certain brand of jeans, for example. However, unless a **benefactor** provides clothing for all students, some parents will buy uniforms at discount stores, and some will buy them at boutiques. The difference between income levels will be more subtle. Still, students will be aware of it.

Some people think a dress code will **repress** gang activity and reduce violence at school by outlawing the wearing of gang colors. Yet gangs might sidestep this rule by changing their outward symbols of membership. Gangs and violence in the schools are a complex problem. It cannot be solved with a dress code.

Will a dress code help build students' self-confidence? This is not likely. Wearing uniforms actually **suppresses** students' self-expression, almost like asking everyone to look the same. In fact, wearing uniforms might harm some students' confidence by forcing them to wear clothing that exaggerates a weight problem, for

example. Instead, schools should encourage students to respect their differences.

Many schools do not have a formal dress code. Still, students know they will be **reprimanded** if they wear T-shirts with certain messages on them or clothing that is too short or too tight. They know they will be disciplined or even sent home if they wear clothing that attracts too much attention. For most students, it's easier to follow the unwritten dress code than to **aggravate** school staff. They save their "wild and crazy" clothes for after school.

Following a dress code is not a **grave** problem for most students like more serious situations, such as losing after-school activities because of school budget cuts. Having a dress code certainly **facilitates** getting dressed in the morning. After all, you don't have to wonder if this shirt goes with those pants. You don't have to make any decisions at all.

Many students who attend schools with dress codes do not feel a **grievous** loss of their rights. They accept wearing uniforms to school. Like rules about not talking during class, a dress code is not meant to **oppress** them but to help them concentrate on their schoolwork.

If your school is considering the adoption of a dress code, study both sides of the issue. Then form your own opinion. Decide whether a dress code at your school would be a step in the right direction—or a stumble.

Practice the Context Clues Strategy Here are two of the boldfaced words from the essay on page 188. Use the context clues strategy you learned in Part 1 on page 183 to figure out the meanings of these words.

suppresses

Read the sentence that uses the word *suppresses* and some of the sentences around it.

Look for context clues to the word's meaning. What clues showing **What the Word Is Compared With** can you find?

_____

Think about the context clues. What other information do you know?

_____

Predict a meaning for the word *suppress*.

_____

Check your Word Wisdom Dictionary to be sure of the meaning of the word *suppress*. Which of the meanings for the word fits the context?

_____

grave

Read the sentence that uses the word *grave* and some of the sentences around it.

Look for context clues to the word's meaning. What clues showing **What the Word Is Compared With** can you find?

_____

Think about the context clues. What other information do you know?

_____

Predict a meaning for the word *grave*.

_____

Check your Word Wisdom Dictionary to be sure of the meaning of the word *grave*. Which of the meanings for the word fits the context?

_____

Unlock the Meanings

Several words you studied in Part 1 have Latin roots. Knowing the meaning of these roots will help you unlock the meanings of many unfamiliar words. Each root can relate to things, qualities, or actions that are either good or bad.

Latin Root: **fac, fic** meaning: to make; to do; easy; face	Latin Root: **grav, grie** meaning: heavy	Latin Root: **press** meaning: to press
English word: *deface* meaning: to ruin the appearance of	English word: *grief* meaning: sorrow; suffering	English word: *depress* meaning: to press down; to make lower in spirits

Categorize by Roots Find these roots in the words in the Word List. Write each word in the correct column. Remember that the spellings of roots can change. Then think of other words you know that come from the same Latin roots. Write each word in the correct column.

WORD LIST

- beneficial
- benefactor
- repress
- suppress
- reprimand
- aggravate
- grave
- facilitate
- grievous
- oppress

Latin Root: **fac, fic**	Latin Root: **grav, grie**	Latin Root: **press**
_____	_____	_____
_____	_____	_____
_____	_____	_____
_____	_____	_____
_____	_____	_____

Good and Bad

Prefix	Meaning
ag-	toward, to, before
op-	against

Example

op- (against) + press (press) = oppress

Use Roots and Prefixes   Circle the root and any prefix you find in the boldfaced words. Use context clues, roots, and prefixes to write the meaning of the word. Remember that the spellings of roots can change. Check your definitions in a dictionary.

1 Unable to **repress** a smile, the reporter told the whole amusing story.

_____

2 Andrew Carnegie, a **benefactor** who helped charities, invested in steel.

_____

3 For some people, a hot bath and warm milk **facilitate** sleep.

_____

4 The jurists had a **grave** decision to make about the case.

_____

5 Dad is tired and grumpy, and loud music is going to **aggravate** him.

_____

6 Our neighbor's dog hides when his owner tries to **reprimand** him.

_____

7 Regular exercise is **beneficial** to health and fitness.

_____

8 The politician tried to **suppress** the gossip about him from being published.

_____

9 Many countries still **oppress** their citizens with cruel and harsh laws.

_____

10 The country suffered a **grievous** loss when an earthquake destroyed its capital.

_____

WORD LIST

- beneficial
- benefactor
- repress
- suppress
- reprimand
- aggravate
- grave
- facilitate
- grievous
- oppress

Choose the Correct Word Write the best word from each pair of words from the Word List to complete each sentence.

1 The scientist made a (grave/beneficial) error in his calculations and ruined his work. _____

2 The family tried to (suppress/oppress) information about the senator's illness out of respect for her privacy. _____

3 Sending in his essays may (aggravate/facilitate) Jim's efforts to get a job at the newspaper. _____

4 Vegetables have nutrients that are (beneficial/benefactor) in fighting infections. _____

5 Throughout history, people have been (aggravated/oppressed) by harsh dictators. _____

6 Kyle suffered a (grievous/beneficial) injury when he broke his leg.

_____

7 The hall monitor (facilitated/reprimanded) the noisy students.

_____

8 Mariah couldn't (repress/oppress) a laugh when she saw that she was wearing two different shoes. _____

9 Carl hopes to find a (benefactor/beneficial) to finance his business idea.

_____

10 Aunt Phoebe says that long lines (aggravate/suppress) her annoyance at shopping. _____

Apply What You've Learned

Demonstrate Word Knowledge Answer each question by writing **Yes** or **No** on the line. Explain the reasons for your choice.

1 Might some people think that obedience training could **suppress** a dog's

personality? _____

2 Would you expect someone to **reprimand** you for doing a good deed?

_____

3 Should a **grave** responsibility be taken lightly? _____

_____

4 If someone **oppresses** other students, is he or she being kind?

_____

5 Would helping someone pack a suitcase **facilitate** his or her leaving?

_____

6 Would you expect to **repress** apples to make cider? _____

_____

7 Might a go-cart's loud engine sounds **aggravate** the neighbors?

_____

8 Would a **benefactor** of the arts contribute toward a new museum?

_____

9 Would a **grievous** occasion be upbeat and cheery? _____

_____

10 Would you expect people to dislike something that is **beneficial** for

everyone? _____

Speak It! Tell your classmates about a time in your life when you turned a bad situation into a good one. Use as many words from the Word List in Part 2 as you can.

PART 3 Reference Skills

for Word Wisdom

A Growing Problem: Unwanted Pets

Every year, more than 12 million dogs and cats end up in animal shelters across the United States. Only about one third of the animals in these shelters will find homes. What should happen to the remaining millions?

The high population of animals in shelters is a growing problem in this country. Animal shelters are drastically overcrowded. Some animals are adopted, but many of them will be put to death. This process is called euthanasia. Shelter staff try to be gentle with this, not **barbaric**. They want to **inflict** as little pain on the animals as possible. Many shelters inject an overdose of a barbiturate into the animal. The dog or cat quickly and painlessly goes to "sleep." Using this method, the workers hold and **console** the animal, reducing its stress.

Other shelters use a different approach. They put the animals into a gas chamber. This method is slower, more dangerous to staff, and more difficult for the animals. Most experts believe that injection is the **superlative** method.

The decision to put an animal down is not difficult if it is very sick, a **menace** to people or other animals, or otherwise unadoptable. Many aggressive animals are acting out of **vengeance** because of previous mistreatment. However, their behavior makes them difficult to place in new homes.

Still, many animals that are euthanized are healthy and friendly. Some have simply become a **nuisance** to their owners, like a broken toy, and end up at a shelter. Should these animals be put to death, too?

Some people think that healthy animals should not be killed but instead should remain at the shelter until they are adopted or die a natural death. "No-kill" shelters do exist. Other shelters are called "low-kill" because only very sick or dangerous animals are put to sleep. There, healthy animals are kept until they are adopted.

However, many people think that this approach is too **optimistic,** like closing your eyes to reality. In fact, these animals are often held in cages for years. They live much longer, but their quality of life, some feel, is **atrocious**.

So how should society deal with millions of unwanted pets? Should most of them be killed, or should they be housed indefinitely? Many communities have programs to spay or neuter cats and dogs. They hope to reduce the number of animals that end up in shelters. Shelter staff and volunteers urge people to adopt animals from shelters. They stress that the experience tends to be **glorious** for both the pet and its new owner.

Imagine that you are in charge of an animal shelter. What would you do with the hundreds of cats and dogs that no one seems to want? It's a heartbreaking issue with both good and bad outcomes.

Practice the Context Clues Strategy   Here are two of the boldfaced words from the essay on page 194. Use the context clues strategy you learned in Part 1 on page 183 to figure out the meanings of these words.

nuisance

📖 **Read** the sentence that uses the word *nuisance* and some of the sentences around it.

🔍 **Look** for context clues to the word's meaning. What clues showing **What the Word Is Compared With** can you find?

_____

💡 **Think** about the context clues. What other information do you know?

_____

➡️ **Predict** a meaning for the word *nuisance*.

_____

✔️ **Check** your Word Wisdom Dictionary to be sure of the meaning of the word *nuisance*. Write the definition here.

_____

optimistic

📖 **Read** the sentence that uses the word *optimistic* and some of the sentences around it.

🔍 **Look** for context clues to the word's meaning. What clues showing **What the Word Is Compared With** can you find?

_____

💡 **Think** about the context clues. What other information do you know?

_____

➡️ **Predict** a meaning for the word *optimistic*.

_____

✔️ **Check** your Word Wisdom Dictionary to be sure of the meaning of the word *optimistic*. Write the definition here.

_____

Unlock the Meanings

Homographs and Homophones When you use a dictionary to find a definition or a spelling, be sure you are checking for the word you really want and need. Some words are so close in pronunciation, meaning, and spelling that they can cause confusion.

Homographs are words that are spelled alike but have different origins and meanings. *Homograph* means "same writing." Homographs often have different pronunciations. For example, the word *console* from the Word List on page 197 can be a verb or a noun. The verb is pronounced /kən sōl'/. It means "to give comfort." The noun is pronounced /kŏn' sōl'/. It means everything from "the keyboard of an organ" to "the control panel for an electronic or mechanical device" to "the raised portion between the bucket seats of a car."

Homophones are words that sound alike but have different meanings and spellings. *Homophone* means "same sound." For example, *toad,* meaning "an amphibian with dry, warty skin," and *towed,* meaning "pulled by a rope, chain, or other device," are homophones.

Identify Homographs and Homophones Identify whether each set of words is a homograph or a homophone. Then explain how to tell the difference between them.

1 wade/weighed _____

_____

2 course/coarse _____

_____

3 tear/tear _____

_____

4 reflects/reflex _____

_____

5 bow/bow/bow _____

_____

_____

_____

Find the Meaning

1. Use context clues.
2. Look for a familiar root, prefix, or suffix.
3. If the context or a word part doesn't help, check the dictionary.

WORD LIST

barbaric
inflict
console
superlative
menace
vengeance
nuisance
optimistic
atrocious
glorious

Define the Words Follow the steps above to write the meaning of each boldfaced word. Write 1, 2, or 3 to show which steps you used.

1 An active curious toddler can be a **menace** in a glassware shop.

_____

2 Some combinations of colors are **atrocious**.

_____

3 We are **optimistic** that Bill will be home from college in time for the holidays.

_____

4 The behavior of the mob was so **barbaric** that someone called the police.

_____

5 Not having a locker is a **nuisance** because we have to carry our book bags.

_____

6 The first flowers of spring are a **glorious** sight after a long, cold winter.

_____

7 The playwright's latest play is the **superlative** achievement of his career.

_____

8 Out of **vengeance** for the attack on their village, the people went to war.

_____

9 We tried to **console** Diana after her team lost the game, but she was still upset.

_____

10 The hurricane **inflicted** serious damage on buildings along the coastline.

_____

Process the Meanings

WORD LIST

barbaric

inflict

console

superlative

menace

vengeance

nuisance

optimistic

atrocious

glorious

Choose the Correct Word Write the word from the Word List that best completes each sentence.

1 His babysitter tried to _____ the unhappy child by singing to him.

2 During our trip, the weather was _____; we drove through snow and sleet the whole time.

3 Kind people try not to _____ pain on others.

4 When the rain stopped, we saw the most _____ double rainbow.

5 People who are cruel and brutal often behave in _____ ways.

6 The oil spill in the harbor was a _____ to the wildlife in the area.

7 It is better to solve problems peacefully than to seek _____.

8 Some people are sad and pessimistic while others are cheerful and _____.

9 Although it kept out bugs, the broken screen door was ugly and a _____.

10 Stacy uses such glowing terms that it's hard to tell when something is just nice and when it is _____.

Complete the Analogies Write the word from the Word List that best completes each analogy.

1 guilty : innocent :: pessimistic : _____

2 rebellion : suppress :: suffering : _____

3 nice : kindness :: dangerous : _____

4 toxin : toxic :: barbarian : _____

Choose the Best Word Write the word from the Word List that best fits each situation.

5 This is something that isn't worth the bother. _____

6 This describes something that is the greatest. _____

7 Offensive behavior, ugly decorations, and terrible crimes can all be described by this adjective. _____

8 The expression "an eye for an eye; a tooth for a tooth" is an example of this noun. _____

9 This is something you might do with kind words to help someone who is grieving. _____

10 This adjective describes something that is full of wonder and beauty.

_____

11 The expression "look on the bright side" is an example of being this.

_____

12 Some pirates were described by this adjective.

_____

Write It! Friendship is a popular theme in books, movies, and songs. Write about the good qualities you like in a friend. Use as many words from the Word List in Part 3 as you can.

Review

for Word Wisdom

Categorize by Connotation Decide whether each word in the Word List has a positive or a negative meaning. Write each word in the correct column. When you are finished, circle every word that has the root *fac, fic; grav, grie;* or *press.* Remember that the spellings of roots can change.

WORD LIST

- staunch
- grudging
- obsession
- pesky
- truce
- deface
- grief
- bias
- faction
- despondent
- beneficial
- benefactor
- repress
- suppress
- reprimand
- aggravate
- grave
- facilitate
- grievous
- oppress
- barbaric
- inflict
- console
- superlative
- menace
- vengeance
- nuisance
- optimistic
- atrocious
- glorious

Positive	Negative

Complete Word Ladders List each group of words in their proper order on the word ladder. Put the most positive word on the top and the most negative word on the bottom.

1 pesky, glorious, barbaric

4 console, oppress, reprimand

2 atrocious, superlative, grave

5 grudging, optimistic, grievous

3 truce, menace, benefactor

Identify Antonyms Circle the word that is an antonym for each vocabulary word in the first column.

6 vengeance   revenge, forgiveness

7 aggravate   irritate, soothe

8 optimistic   negative, positive

9 suppress   release, hold

10 grief   sorrow, joy

Taking Vocabulary Tests

TEST-TAKING STRATEGY

Some vocabulary tests ask you to define a word in the context of a short paragraph. Read the paragraph carefully. Think of a meaning for the boldfaced word before you read the answer choices. Then read the choices and decide whether the meaning you thought of is a possible choice. Recheck your answer by substituting it for the boldfaced word. Make sure your choice makes sense in the context of the paragraph.

Sample:

As hard as I try, I have trouble speaking in class. Whatever the topic, I can't seem to find the right words. Even if I am only answering a question, I keep saying *um, uh, you know,* and *like*. No matter how hard I try to **repress** these disruptive words, I can't seem to say a sentence without them.

The word **repress** in this paragraph is best defined as

○ understand
○ replace
● hold back
○ excuse

Practice Test   Fill in the circle of the answer choice that best defines the boldfaced word as it is used in the paragraph.

1   Second to highway accidents, falls cause the most accidental deaths. Though you may feel that the following precautions are **nuisances**, they can save a life. Wipe up spills so that people don't slip on a wet floor. Keep stairs and hallways well lighted. Most falls can be prevented.

The word **nuisances** in this paragraph is best defined as

○ pests   ○ experiences   ○ insects   ○ annoyances

2   The *blog*, a blended form of the words *web log*, has become popular. This kind of journal writing gives the average person a chance to reach many others online. What is particularly **beneficial** about these websites is that you can always find someone who shares similar ideas.

The word **beneficial** in this paragraph is best defined as

○ helpful   ○ kind   ○ disturbing   ○ cheerful

3   Long ago, many quilts of **superlative** quality were made out of whatever was available. Patchworks of old jeans, cornmeal sacks, and burlap were sewn together for warmth and comfort. These quilts are also works of art. Spare and simple, they have an eye-catching abstract quality.

The word **superlative** in this paragraph is best defined as

○ the most   ○ the highest   ○ the least   ○ the lowest

4   Iron is one of the trace minerals. These minerals are needed in the diet in small daily amounts. Meats, fish, poultry, and beans are rich in iron. People who do not get enough iron feel tired and weak. They may get headaches and feel **despondent**. Children and teenagers sometimes need iron supplements because they grow so quickly.

The word **despondent** in this paragraph is best defined as

○ lacking   ○ limited   ○ skilled   ○ sad

5   Like golf, croquet involves hitting a ball at a target with a club or mallet. A croquet game consists of scoring points by hitting colored balls through a series of arches, or wickets, in a certain order. **Staunch** fans and defenders of this sport have encouraged its revival.

The word **staunch** in this paragraph is best defined as

○ strong   ○ loyal   ○ ancient   ○ proud

Build New Words

Add Suffixes When you add a suffix to a word, the new word may have a similar meaning, but it usually functions as a different part of speech.

> **Suffixes That Form Adjectives**
> The suffix -*ive* means "having a tendency to."
> The suffix -*ous* means "full of."

Change the vocabulary words in the chart below. Subtract letters as shown. Then add the suffix to change each vocabulary word into a new word. Write the part of speech of the new word.

Vocabulary Word	Minus	+ Suffix	= New Word	Part of Speech
faction	-on	-ous		
repress		-ive		
obsession	-ion	-ive		
oppress		-ive		
barbaric	-ic	-ous		

Speak It! What do you think is meant by the term "growing up"? Talk about the process of growing up and give your opinion about its good and bad sides. Use as many words from the Word List in Part 4 as you can.

Word Wisdom Dictionary

PRONUNCIATION KEY

/ă/	pat
/ā/	pay
/â/	care
/ä/	father
/är/	far
/ĕ/	pet
/ē/	be
/ĭ/	pit
/ī/	pie
/îr/	pier
/ŏ/	mop
/ō/	toe
/ô/	paw, for
/oi/	noise
/ou/	out
/o͝o/	look
/o͞o/	boot
/ŭ/	cut
/ûr/	urge
/th/	thin
/th/	this
/hw/	what
/zh/	vision
/ə/	about
	item
	pencil
	gallop
	circus
/ər/	butter

A

ab•o•rig•i•nal /ăb′ ə rĭj′ ə nəl/ *adj.* existing from the beginning; relating to aborigines. *We studied aboriginal cultures.* —**ab•o•rig•in•al•ly** *adv.*

ab•o•rig•i•ne /ăb′ ə rĭj′ ə nē/ *n.* a member of the first people to live in an area. *The aborigines of Australia were hunters.*

ac•quaint /ə kwānt′/ *v.* **ac•quaint•ed, ac•quaint•ing, ac•quaints.** to make something known; to inform. *My father acquainted me with cooking skills.*

ac•quain•tance /ə kwān′ təns/ *n.* a person one knows. *She is a recent acquaintance of mine.* —**ac•quain•tance•ship** *n.*

ad•vo•cate¹ /ăd′ və kĭt *or* ād′ və kāt′/ *n.* a supporter or defender. *John is a strong advocate of animal rights.* —**ad•vo•ca•tion** *n.* —**ad•vo•ca•tor** *n.*

ad•vo•cate² /ăd′ və kĭt *or* ād′ və kāt′/ *n.* a person who practices law. *The advocate supported his client at the trial.* —**ad•vo•ca•tion** *n.* —**ad•vo•ca•tor** *n.*

ad•vo•cate³ /ăd′ və kāt′/ *v.* **ad•vo•cat•ed, ad•vo•cat•ing, ad•vo•cates.** to be in favor of something. *Amy advocates new laws for the protection of the environment.* —**ad•vo•ca•tion** *n.* —**ad•vo•ca•tor** *n.*

af•flic•tion¹ /ə flĭk′ shən/ *n.* pain or discomfort. *His affliction made walking difficult.*

af•flic•tion² /ə flĭk′ shən/ *n.* something causing pain or discomfort. *Smallpox was a deadly affliction.*

ag•gra•vate¹ /ăg′ rə vāt′/ *v.* **ag•gra•vat•ed, ag•gra•vat•ing, ag•gra•vates.** to make something worse than it was. *Scratching the sore will aggravate it.* —**ag•gra•vat•ing•ly** *adv.* —**ag•gra•va•tor** *n.*

ag•gra•vate² /ăg′ rə vāt′/ *v.* **ag•gra•vat•ed, ag•gra•vat•ing, ag•gra•vates.** to annoy; to irritate. *Interruptions aggravate me when I am working.* —**ag•gra•vat•ing•ly** *adv.* —**ag•gra•va•tor** *n.*

al•ien•ate /āl′ yə nāt′ *or* ā′ lē ə nāt′/ *v.* **al•ien•at•ed, al•ien•at•ing, al•ien•ates.** to cause to be unfriendly. *His rude behavior alienated many people.* —**al•ien•a•tor** *n.*

al•li•ance /ə lī′ əns/ *n.* an agreement formed between people, organizations, or countries. *Our country has an alliance with the United Kingdom.*

al•ly¹ /ə lī′ *or* ăl′ ī/ *v.* **al•lied, al•ly•ing, al•lies.** to unite for a purpose; to support. *Political figures usually ally themselves with a political party.*

al•ly² /ăl′ ī *or* ə lī′/ *n., pl.* **al•lies.** one who is supportive of another. *We can count on Jean to be our ally.*

am•ble¹ /ăm′ bəl/ *v.* **am•bled, am•bling, am•bles.** to walk slowly in a carefree manner. *Visitors amble through the beautiful garden.* —**am•bler** *n.*

am•ble² /ăm′ bəl/ *n.* a leisurely pace of walking. *His amble convinced us that he did not need to hurry to the meeting.*

an•nu•al¹ /ăn′ yōō əl/ *adj.* taking place each year; yearly. *Our fall festival is an annual event.* —**an•nu•al•ly** *adv.*

an•nu•al² /ăn′ yōō əl/ *n.* a yearbook; something published yearly. *Our school publishes an annual with all the students' pictures in it.*

an•nu•al³ /ăn′ yōō əl/ *n.* a plant that lives one season. *We know that these flowers will die during the winter because they are annuals.*

an•tic•i•pate /ăn tĭs′ ə pāt′/ *v.* **an•tic•i•pat•ed, an•tic•i•pat•ing, an•tic•i•pates.** to expect; to look forward to. *I anticipate having a good time with my cousins.* —**an•tic•i•pa•tor** *n.*

a•pol•o•get•ic /ə pŏl′ ə jĕt′ ĭk/ *adj.* behaving as though one is sorry; showing regret. *His apologetic manner helped end the argument.* —**a•pol•o•get•i•cal•ly** *adv.*

a•pol•o•gy /ə pŏl′ ə jē/ *n., pl.* **a•pol•o•gies.** a stated or written expression of regret. *I wrote a letter of apology for my behavior.*

ar•ti•fi•cial /är′ tə fĭsh′ əl/ *adj.* made by humans; not a natural occurrence. *An artificial leg helped John walk.* —**ar•ti•fi•cial•ly** *adv.* —**ar•ti•fi•ci•al•i•ty** /är′ tə fĭsh′ ē ăl′ ĭ tē/ *n.*

as•pi•rate /ăs′ pə rāt′/ *v.* **as•pi•rat•ed, as•pi•rat•ing, as•pi•rates.** to remove an obstruction by suctioning. *The doctor aspirated the water from the boy's air passages.*

a•tro•cious /ə trō′ shəs/ *adj.* horrible; very bad. *He was convicted of an atrocious crime.* —**a•tro•cious•ly** *adv.* —**a•tro•cious•ness** *n.*

at•tain /ə tān′/ *v.* **at•tained, at•tain•ing, at•tains.** to reach; to achieve. *I can attain my goal if I am willing to work hard.* —**at•tain•a•ble** *adj.* —**at•tain•a•bil•i•ty** *n.* —**at•tain•a•ble•ness** *n.*

at•ten•tive¹ /ə tĕn′ tĭv/ *adj.* paying attention; watchful. *The students were attentive as the principal spoke.* —**at•ten•tive•ly** *adv.* —**at•ten•tive•ness** *n.*

at•ten•tive² /ə tĕn′ tĭv/ *adj.* considerate or thoughtful. *I was attentive to my mother's needs when she had the flu last month.* —**at•ten•tive•ly** *adv.* —**at•ten•tive•ness** *n.*

au•dac•i•ty¹ /ô dăs′ ĭ tē/ *n., pl.* **au•dac•i•ties.** fearless daring. *The diver's audacity enabled him to set new records.*

au•dac•i•ty² /ô dăs′ ĭ tē/ *n., pl.* **au•dac•i•ties.** an act of speaking or behaving in a brash manner. *The student's audacity got her in trouble.*

au•di•ble /ô′ də bəl/ *adj.* loud enough to be heard. *The music from the band room was audible from the hall.* —**au•di•bly** *adv.* —**au•di•bil•i•ty** *n.* —**au•di•ble•ness** *n.*

au•di•o¹ /ô′ dē ō′/ *adj.* having to do with sound. *Because of a problem with the audio equipment, we missed the last song.*

au•di•o² /ô′ dē ō′/ *n., pl.* **au•di•os.** the sending, copying, or receiving of sounds. *The new speakers improved the audio of my stereo.*

au•di•tion¹ /ô dĭsh′ ən/ *n.* a performance used as a test. *The audition determines who will be chosen for the orchestra.*

au•di•tion² /ô dĭsh′ ən/ *v.* **au•di•tioned, au•di•tion•ing, au•di•tions.** to perform in order to obtain employment or a position. *Several students will audition for the lead role in the school play.*

au•di•to•ry /ô′ dĭ tôr′ ē/ *adj.* having to do with the sense of hearing. *An infection caused Bob to have an auditory problem.*

au•then•tic /ô thĕn′ tĭk/ *adj.* genuine; real. *The buried jewels were authentic.* —**au•then•ti•cal•ly** *adv.*

bar•bar•i•an¹ /bär bâr′ ē ən/ *n.* a person from a group that is looked upon as uncivilized or savage. *The explorers found it difficult to communicate with the barbarians.*

bar•bar•i•an[2] /bär **bâr′** ē ən/ *n.* a crude, fierce, or brutal person. *The village was attacked by thousands of barbarians.*

bar•bar•ic /bär **băr′** ĭk/ *adj.* unacceptable; crude. *An acceptable custom in one country may seem barbaric in another.*

bar•ba•rous /**bär′** bər əs/ *adj.* uncivilized. *The leader was known for his barbarous rule.*

ben•e•fac•tor /**běn′** ə făk′ tər/ *n.* a person who helps others through financial or other aid. *The benefactor donated money to cancer research.*

ben•e•fi•cial /běn′ ə **fĭsh′** əl/ *adj.* helpful; favorable; causing improvement. *The extra practice was beneficial to the team.* —**ben•e•fi•cial•ly** *adv.* —**ben•e•fi•cial•ness** *n.*

ben•e•fit[1] /**běn′** ə fĭt/ *n.* something helpful; an advantage. *A good education will be a great benefit to you.*

ben•e•fit[2] /**běn′** ə fĭt/ *n.* a public event held to raise money for a person or cause. *We held a benefit to raise money for the hospital.*

ben•e•fit[3] /**běn′** ə fĭt/ *v.* **ben•e•fit•ed, ben•e•fit•ing, ben•e•fits** or **ben•e•fit•ted, ben•e•fit•ting, ben•e•fits.** to be helpful. *The teacher's help will benefit our science project.*

be•nign /bĭ **nīn′**/ *adj.* of no danger to health; not malignant. *We were happy to find out that the tumor was benign.* —**be•nign•ly** *adv.*

bi•as[1] /**bī′** əs/ *n., pl.* **bi•as•es.** a diagonal direction on cloth that is woven. *We can cut this cloth on the bias.*

bi•as[2] /**bī′** əs/ *n., pl.* **bi•as•es.** a feeling for or against something without enough reason; a prejudice. *He loves cats but has no bias against dogs.*

bi•as[3] /**bī′** əs/ *v.* **bi•ased, bi•as•ing, bi•as•es** or **bi•assed, bi•as•sing, bi•as•ses.** to cause to have a prejudiced view. *This information would bias the jury and make the trial unfair.*

bi•o•sphere /**bī′** ə sfîr′/ *n.* the part of the earth in which life exists. *Earth's biosphere includes its land, water, and air.*

bi•zarre /bĭ **zär′**/ *adj.* odd or unexpected in appearance, style, or character. *The dancers wore bizarre costumes.*

C

cal•i•pers /**kăl′** ə pərs/ *pl., n.* an instrument, with two hinged legs, for measuring thickness or diameter. *We used calipers to measure the thickness of the pottery.*

can•did[1] /**kăn′** dĭd/ *adj.* open and direct; straightforward. *He was candid with his answers.* —**can•did•ly** *adv.* —**can•did•ness** *n.*

can•did[2] /**kăn′** dĭd/ *adj.* without posing or rehearsing. *My mom took some candid photographs at my birthday party.* —**can•did•ly** *adv.* —**can•did•ness** *n.*

cap•ti•vat•ing /**kăp′** tĭ vāt′ ĭng/ *adj.* attracting the attention or affection of. *The dance performance was captivating.* —**cap•ti•va•tion** *n.*

cas•cade[1] /kă **skād′**/ *v.* **cas•cad•ed, cas•cad•ing, cas•cades.** to fall or drop. *The water cascaded off the roof during the storm.*

cas•cade[2] /kă **skād′**/ *n.* a waterfall or series of small waterfalls. *The beautiful cascade brought many tourists to the river resort.*

cav•ern /**kăv′** ərn/ *n.* a large cave. *We like to explore the cavern in the park.*

cav•ern•ous /**kăv′** ər nəs/ *adj.* like a cavern; huge. *The fruit cellar is cavernous.*

cease /sēs/ *v.* **ceased, ceas•ing, ceas•es.** to stop; to come to an end. *My father said the rain would soon cease.*

cease•less /**sēs′** lĭs/ *adj.* endless; constant. *The interruptions to our work seemed ceaseless.* —**cease•less•ly** *adv.* —**cease•less•ness** *n.*

chan•de•lier /shăn′ də **lîr′**/ *n.* a light fixture that holds many bulbs and hangs from the ceiling. *The chandelier in the castle was covered with dust.*

PRONUNCIATION KEY	
/ă/	pat
/ā/	pay
/â/	care
/ä/	father
/är/	far
/ĕ/	pet
/ē/	be
/ĭ/	pit
/ī/	pie
/îr/	pier
/ŏ/	mop
/ō/	toe
/ô/	paw, for
/oi/	noise
/ou/	out
/ŏŏ/	look
/ōō/	boot
/ŭ/	cut
/ûr/	urge
/th/	thin
/th/	this
/hw/	what
/zh/	vision
/ə/	about
	item
	pencil
	gallop
	circus
/ər/	butter

chro•mat•ic /krō măt′ ĭk/ *adj.* relating to color. *A color wheel is a chromatic chart.* —**chro•mat•i•cal•ly** *adv.*

co•in•cide¹ /kō′ ĭn sīd′/ *v.* **co•in•cid•ed, co•in•cid•ing, co•in•cides.** to take place at the same time. *Unfortunately, my baseball and soccer practices coincided.*

co•in•cide² /kō′ ĭn sīd′/ *v.* **co•in•cid•ed, co•in•cid•ing, co•in•cides.** to agree. *My opinion usually coincides with the opinion of my parents.*

col•lo•qui•al /kə lō′ kwē əl/ *adj.* informal or conversational. *Our teacher prefers that colloquial speech not be used in our papers.* —**col•lo•qui•al•ly** *adv.* —**col•lo•qui•al•ness** *n.*

com•mit¹ /kə mĭt′/ *v.* **com•mit•ted, com•mit•ting, com•mits.** to promise or obligate oneself. *Don will commit his time to this task.* —**com•mit•ta•ble** *adj.*

com•mit² /kə mĭt′/ *v.* **com•mit•ted, com•mit•ting, com•mits.** to do or perform; to perpetrate. *A jury must decide if he committed the crime.* —**com•mit•ta•ble** *adj.*

com•mit•ment¹ /kə mĭt′ mənt/ *n.* a promise or pledge. *Our commitment is to complete the work before it's due.*

com•mit•ment² /kə mĭt′ mənt/ *n.* an emotional tie to another. *Our family members have a strong commitment to each other.*

com•mu•nal /kə myōō′ nəl/ *adj.* something shared and used by a number of people. *The city set aside land for a communal garden.* —**com•mu•nal•ly** *adv.*

com•mune¹ /kə myōōn′/ *v.* **com•muned, com•mun•ing, com•munes.** to feel close to. *I commune with nature when I watch a sunset.*

com•mune² /kŏm′ yōōn′ or kə myōōn′/ *n.* a small community whose members share property. *Many experimental communes have been started in the United States.*

com•plex•ion /kəm plĕk′ shən/ *n.* the skin tones or appearance of skin; the way things appear. *Alisa has a creamy brown complexion.*

com•pli•ant /kəm plī′ ənt/ *adj.* willing to agree or go along with the requests of others. *A successful business must be compliant with its customers' requests.* —**com•pli•ant•ly** *adv.*

com•ply /kəm plī′/ *v.* **com•plied, com•ply•ing, com•plies.** to follow a request; to follow rules. *Every team must comply with the rules of the game.*

com•press¹ /kəm prĕs′/ *v.* **com•pressed, com•press•ing, com•press•es.** to make something take less space; to press or squeeze together. *We compress the cans before we recycle them.*

com•press² /kŏm′ prĕs′/ *n., pl.* **com•press•es.** cotton or other material that can be applied to an injury. *A cold compress can reduce swelling.*

com•press•i•ble /kəm prĕs′ ə bəl/ *adj.* able to be made smaller or squeezed together. *The compressible raft was easy to pack.*

con•ceit•ed /kən sē′ tĭd/ *adj.* having an overly high opinion of oneself or one's appearance. *The conceited track star was shocked to have lost the race.* —**con•ceit•ed•ly** *adv.* —**con•ceit•ed•ness** *n.*

con•crete¹ /kŏn krēt′ or kŏn′ krēt′/ *adj.* particular; relating to a particular thing. *Is there a concrete plan for the event?* —**con•crete•ly** *adv.* —**con•crete•ness** *n.*

con•crete² /kŏn′ krēt′ or kŏn krēt′/ *n.* a material made of sand, stone, and cement. *The workers poured concrete for the sidewalk.*

con•de•scend•ing /kŏn′ dĭ sĕn′ dĭng/ *adj.* displaying a superior attitude. *The performers were condescending toward those less talented.* —**con•de•scend•ing•ly** *adv.*

con•sec•u•tive /kən sĕk′ yə tĭv/ *adj.* following in order and without interruption. *I had a hit in five consecutive baseball games.* —**con•sec•u•tive•ly** *adv.* —**con•sec•u•tive•ness** *n.*

con•sole¹ /kən sōl′/ *v.* **con•soled, con•sol•ing, con•soles.** to give comfort. *I will console Jane while we search for her dog.*

con•sole² /kŏn′ sōl′/ *n.* a stand or cabinet for holding a television or sound system. *We bought a console to hold our new stereo.*

con•sti•tu•tion¹ /kŏn′ stĭ tōō′ shən/ *n.* the physical character or makeup of a person. *Mike's strong constitution helped him stay healthy.*

con•sti•tu•tion² /kŏn′ stĭ too′ shən/ *n.* the laws or principles used to govern a country or organization. *Each of our states developed its own constitution.*

con•tent•ed /kən tĕn′ tĭd/ *adj.* satisfied. *The contented dog slept peacefully.*
—**con•tent•ed•ly** *adv.*
—**con•tent•ed•ness** *n.*

con•ten•tious /kən tĕn′ shəs/ *adj.* ready to argue; disagreeable. *The contentious clerk was not willing to listen.*
—**con•ten•tious•ly** *adv.*
—**con•ten•tious•ness** *n.*

con•tin•ue¹ /kən tĭn′ yoo/ *v.* **con•tin•ued, con•tin•u•ing, con•tin•ues.** to go on. *I will continue working on the report.*
—**con•tin•u•a•ble** *adj.*

con•tin•ue² /kən tĭn′ yoo/ *v.* **con•tin•ued, con•tin•u•ing, con•tin•ues.** to last; to remain. *How long will this new trend continue?* —**con•tin•u•a•ble** *adj.*

con•tin•ue³ /kən tĭn′ yoo/ *v.* **con•tin•ued, con•tin•u•ing, con•tin•ues.** to resume after an interruption. *I continued with my reading when I got off the phone.*
—**con•tin•u•a•ble** *adj.*

con•tin•u•ous /kən tĭn′ yoo əs/ *adj.* without interruption; unbroken. *We depend on a continuous supply of electricity.*
—**con•tin•u•ous•ly** *adv.*
—**con•tin•u•ous•ness** *n.*

con•vo•ca•tion /kŏn′ və kā′ shən/ *n.* a group united for a particular purpose. *A convocation of school leaders held an important meeting.*

cor•po•ral¹ /kôr′ pər əl or kôr′ prəl/ *adj.* having to do with the body. *Most psychologists oppose corporal punishment.*

cor•po•ral² /kôr′ pər əl or kôr′ prəl/ *n.* a military ranking in the U.S. Army, Air Force, and Marine Corps. *The army corporal hoped for a promotion soon.*

corps /kôr/ *n., pl.* **corps** /kôrz/. a group of people working together. *The president is often followed by a corps of reporters.*

corpse /kôrps/ *n.* a dead body; usually referring to a human. *The corpse was examined before being moved.*

cor•set /kôr′ sĭt/ *n.* a tight-fitting undergarment worn to enhance appearance. *The actors wore corsets under their costumes.*

cos•mic /kŏz′ mĭk/ *adj.* having to do with the universe; vast. *Storms on the surface of the sun are a cosmic event.*
—**cos•mi•cal•ly** *adv.*

cre•vasse /krĭ văs′/ *n.* a deep chasm. *The crevasse in the ice is dangerous.*

cur•rent¹ /kûr′ ənt or kŭr′ ənt/ *adj.* presently accepted; up-to-date. *The new telephone book has a list of current numbers.*
—**cur•rent•ly** *adv.* —**cur•rent•ness** *n.*

cur•rent² /kûr′ ənt or kŭr′ ənt/ *n.* the flow of liquid or gas. *We could feel a current of warm air when we opened the door.*

cur•rent³ /kûr′ ənt or kŭr′ ənt/ *n.* the flow of electric charge. *We needed enough current to run a clothes dryer.*

cy•clone /sī′ klōn′/ *n.* a storm with strong, destructive winds that move in a circular motion. *My family prepared for the approaching cyclone.*
—**cy•clon•ic** /sī klŏn′ ĭk/ *adj.*

D

de•ceit•ful /dĭ sēt′ fəl/ *adj.* misleading; not truthful. *The deceitful employee claimed he was too ill to come to work.*
—**de•ceit•ful•ly** *adv.* —**de•ceit•ful•ness** *n.*

de•cent¹ /dē′ sənt/ *adj.* following proper standards of behavior; acceptable. *Decent people follow the law.* —**de•cent•ly** *adv.*
—**de•cent•ness** *n.*

de•cent² /dē′ sənt/ *adj.* considerate; kind. *Jennifer behaved in a decent manner.*
—**de•cent•ly** *adv.* —**de•cent•ness** *n.*

dé•cor or **de•cor** /dā′ kôr′ or dā kôr′/ *n.* the style used in furnishing a room. *We wanted the décor to reflect our interest in sports.*

de•face /dĭ fās′/ *v.* **de•faced, de•fac•ing, de•fac•es.** to ruin the appearance of. *Who defaced the monument in the park?*
—**de•face•a•ble** *adj.* —**de•face•ment** *n.*
—**de•fac•er** *n.*

PRONUNCIATION KEY

/ă/	pat
/ā/	pay
/â/	care
/ä/	father
/är/	far
/ĕ/	pet
/ē/	be
/ĭ/	pit
/ī/	pie
/îr/	pier
/ŏ/	mop
/ō/	toe
/ô/	paw, for
/oi/	noise
/ou/	out
/oo/	look
/oo/	boot
/ŭ/	cut
/ûr/	urge
/th/	thin
/th/	this
/hw/	what
/zh/	vision
/ə/	about
	item
	pencil
	gallop
	circus
/ər/	butter

de•fen•sive¹ /dĭ fĕn′ sĭv/ *adj.* protective of oneself. *She became very defensive when asked about her homework.* —**de•fen•sive•ly** *adv.* —**de•fen•sive•ness** *n.*

de•fen•sive² /dĭ fĕn′ sĭv/ *adj.* intended to avoid attack or danger. *The military unit had a defensive strategy.* —**de•fen•sive•ly** *adv.* —**de•fen•sive•ness** *n.*

def•er•ence /dĕf′ ər əns *or* dĕf′ rəns/ *n.* courteous respect. *The students behaved with deference toward the visitor.*

def•er•en•tial /dĕf′ ə rĕn′ shəl/ *adj.* respectful. *The deferential attitude of the children pleased their parents.* —**def•er•en•tial•ly** *adv.*

de•flect /dĭ flĕkt′/ *v.* **de•flect•ed, de•flect•ing, de•flects.** to turn or cause to turn in another direction; to bend. *The net deflected the tennis ball.* —**de•flect•a•ble** *adj.* —**de•flec•tive** *adj.* —**de•flec•tor** *n.*

de•ploy /dĭ ploi′/ *v.* **de•ployed, de•ploy•ing, de•ploys.** to place in order to be ready for combat; to strategically place or act. *The general deployed his troops.* —**de•ploy•ment** *n.*

de•ploy•a•ble /dĭ ploi′ ə bəl/ *adj.* strategically placed and ready for combat. *The army was deployable upon command.*

de•sen•si•tize /dē sĕn′ sĭ tīz′/ *v.* **de•sen•si•tized, de•sen•si•tiz•ing, de•sen•si•tiz•es.** to decrease a reaction. *Allergy shots can desensitize most allergic children.* —**de•sen•si•tiz•er** *n.*

des•pi•ca•ble /dĕs′ pĭ kə bəl *or* dĭ spĭk′ ə bəl/ *adj.* deserving of contempt; hateful. *Everyone was astonished by his despicable behavior.* —**des•pi•ca•bly** *adv.* —**des•pi•ca•ble•ness** *n.*

de•spon•dent /dĭ spŏn′ dənt/ *adj.* extremely depressed. *The funeral put everyone in a despondent mood.* —**de•spon•dence** *n.* —**de•spon•den•cy** *n.*

de•ter /dĭ tûr′/ *v.* **de•terred, de•ter•ring, de•ters.** to prevent or discourage an action; to stop. *A flat tire will deter his prompt arrival.* —**de•ter•ment** *n.*

de•ter•mine¹ /dĭ tûr′ mĭn/ *v.* **de•ter•mined, de•ter•min•ing, de•ter•mines.** to decide; to conclude. *The referee will determine which team should get the ball.*

de•ter•mine² /dĭ tûr′ mĭn/ *v.* **de•ter•mined, de•ter•min•ing, de•ter•mines.** to be the cause of. *Effort can often determine one's grades.*

de•ter•mine³ /dĭ tûr′ mĭn/ *v.* **de•ter•mined, de•ter•min•ing, de•ter•mines.** to limit. *Time will determine how detailed our report will be.*

dif•fuse¹ /dĭ fyo͞oz′/ *v.* **dif•fused, dif•fus•ing, dif•fus•es.** to spread or scatter. *Smells from the kitchen diffused throughout the house.* —**dif•fus•i•ble** *adj.* —**dif•fuse•ly** *adv.* —**dif•fuse•ness** *n.*

dif•fuse² /dĭ fyo͞oz′/ *v.* **dif•fused, dif•fus•ing, dif•fus•es.** to soften or make less bright. *A filter over your camera lens can diffuse the light.* —**dif•fus•i•ble** *adj.* —**dif•fuse•ly** *adv.* —**dif•fuse•ness** *n.*

dif•fus•i•ble /dĭ fyo͞o′ zə bəl/ *adj.* able to be spread or scattered; able to soften or make less brilliant. *One diffusible light was enough to brighten the entire room.*

di•gress /dī grĕs′ *or* dĭ grĕs′/ *v.* **di•gressed, di•gress•ing, di•gress•es.** to turn aside from the main topic. *Uncle Arnie's stories are sometimes long because he digresses.*

dis•course¹ /dĭs′ kôrs′/ *n.* a friendly talk. *We had a nice discourse over dinner.*

dis•course² /dĭs′ kôrs′/ *n.* a discussion, either written or spoken, of a formal nature. *The speaker's discourse on animals in the wild was fascinating.*

dis•fig•ure /dĭs fĭg′ yər/ *v.* **dis•fig•ured, dis•fig•ur•ing, dis•fig•ures.** to damage the appearance of something. *It is against the law to disfigure public property.*

du•ra•ble /do͝or′ ə bəl *or* dyo͝or′ ə bəl/ *adj.* lasting; able to withstand wear. *Tile is a durable material.* —**du•ra•bly** *adv.* —**du•ra•bil•i•ty** *n.* —**du•ra•ble•ness** *n.*

du•ra•tion /do͝o rā′ shən *or* dyo͝o rā′ shən/ *n.* the time that something exists. *We stayed inside for the duration of the storm.*

ec•o•sys•tem /ĕk′ ō sĭs′ təm *or* ē′ kō sĭs′ təm/ *n.* the community of plants and animals in a geographic region. *A desert would not be a good ecosystem for fish.*

e•ject /ĭ jĕkt′/ *v.* **e•ject•ed, e•ject•ing, e•jects.** to throw or force out; to get rid of. *The referee chose to eject the unruly player.*

e•ject•a•ble /ĭ jĕkt′ ə bəl/ *adj.* able to be thrown out, forced out, or gotten rid of. *The ejectable seat saved the pilot's life.*

el•o•cu•tion /ĕl′ ə kyōō′ shən/ *n.* public speaking that emphasizes good delivery and gestures. *Before making his speech, Joe worked to improve his elocution.*

e•lon•gate /ĭ lông′ gāt′/ *v.* **e•lon•gat•ed, e•lon•gat•ing, e•lon•gates.** to lengthen. *The balloon elongated as it became filled with air.* —**e•lon•gat•ed** *adj.*

el•o•quent¹ /ĕl′ ə kwənt/ *adj.* powerful or moving. *The candidate's eloquent speech won him many votes.* —**el•o•quent•ly** *adv.* —**el•o•quent•ness** *n.*

el•o•quent² /ĕl′ ə kwənt/ *adj.* expressive in a visual way. *The expression on her face was eloquent.* —**el•o•quent•ly** *adv.* —**el•o•quent•ness** *n.*

en•dure¹ /ĕn dŏŏr′ *or* ĕn dyŏŏr′/ *v.* **en•dured, en•dur•ing, en•dures.** to put up with; to bear. *Sometimes I endure my brother's teasing.*

en•dure² /ĕn dŏŏr′ *or* ĕn dyŏŏr′/ *v.* **en•dured, en•dur•ing, en•dures.** to continue to exist; to last. *Redwood trees can endure for thousands of years.*

e•vac•u•ate /ĭ văk′ yōō āt′/ *v.* **e•vac•u•at•ed, e•vac•u•at•ing, e•vac•u•ates.** to go or send away; to empty. *We evacuate the building at the sound of a fire alarm.* —**e•vac•u•a•tor** *n.*

ev•o•ca•tion /ĕv′ ə kā′ shən/ *n.* the creation of a mental response. *The smell of cut grass causes an evocation of summer.*

e•voc•a•tive /ĭ vŏk′ ə tĭv/ *adj.* having the power to create a mental response. *This music is evocative of my Mexican vacation.*

e•voke /ĭ vōk′/ *v.* **e•voked, e•vok•ing, e•vokes.** to create a mental response. *The picture evoked memories of visiting my grandparents.* —**ev•o•ca•ble** *adj.*

e•volve /ĭ vŏlv′/ *v.* **e•volved, e•volv•ing, e•volves.** to develop or change slowly. *New medicines have evolved through skilled research.* —**e•volv•a•ble** *adj.* —**e•volve•ment** *n.*

ex•ag•ger•ate¹ /ĭg zăj′ ə rāt′/ *v.* **ex•ag•ger•at•ed, ex•ag•ger•at•ing, ex•ag•ger•ates.** to overstate or make something seem more important than it is. *Tall tales exaggerate the accomplishments of their characters.* —**ex•ag•ger•a•tive** *adj.* —**ex•ag•ger•a•to•ry** *adj.* —**ex•ag•ger•at•ed•ly** *adv.* —**ex•ag•ger•a•tion** *n.*

ex•ag•ger•ate² /ĭg zăj′ ə rāt′/ *v.* **ex•ag•ger•at•ed, ex•ag•ger•at•ing, ex•ag•ger•ates.** to increase more than is considered normal. *The exaggerated workouts left some of the team members exhausted.* —**ex•ag•ger•a•tive** *adj.* —**ex•ag•ger•a•to•ry** *adj.* —**ex•ag•ger•at•ed•ly** *adv.* —**ex•ag•ger•a•tion** *n.*

ex•ag•ger•a•tion /ĭg zăj′ ə rā′ shən/ *n.* something that is overstated or made more important than it is. *It would be an exaggeration to say that I am starving to death.*

ex•ceed /ĭk sēd′/ *v.* **ex•ceed•ed, ex•ceed•ing, ex•ceeds.** to go beyond a set standard. *We should not exceed the speed limit.*

ex•hale /ĕks hāl′ *or* ĕk sāl′/ *v.* **ex•haled, ex•hal•ing, ex•hales.** to breathe out; to release air from the lungs. *While practicing yoga, Amy counted to ten as she exhaled.*

ex•ot•ic /ĭg zŏt′ ĭk/ *adj.* unusual because of being from another place; unfamiliar or strange. *The exotic flowers needed a lot of care to survive.* —**ex•ot•i•cal•ly** *adv.* —**ex•ot•ic•ness** *n.*

ex•pire /ĭk spīr′/ *v.* **ex•pired, ex•pir•ing, ex•pires.** to end. *My library card expired last month.*

ex•ude /ĭg zo͞od′ *or* ĭk so͞od′/ *v.* **ex•ud•ed, ex•ud•ing, ex•udes.** to exhibit in abundance. *The children exuded energy.*

F

fa•cil•i•tate /fə sĭl′ ĭ tāt′/ *v.* **fa•cil•i•tat•ed, fa•cil•i•tat•ing, fa•cil•i•tates.** to make easier. *These folders facilitate keeping our papers in order.* —**fa•cil•i•ta•tion** *n.*

fac•tion[1] /făk′ shən/ *n.* a small group with ideas different from the larger group's ideas. *One faction of our class did not want to go on the trip.*

fac•tion[2] /făk′ shən/ *n.* a disagreement. *A faction developed during the meeting.*

fac•tious /făk′ shəs/ *adj.* relating to a disagreement. *The factious discussion had her upset all day.* —**fac•tious•ly** *adv.* —**fac•tious•ness** *n.*

flex•i•ble /flĕk′ sə bəl/ *adj.* able to be changed or adjusted; adaptable. *My schedule is flexible.* —**flex•i•bly** *adv.* —**flex•i•bil•i•ty** *n.* —**flex•i•ble•ness** *n.*

fluc•tu•ate /flŭk′ cho͞o āt′/ *v.* **fluc•tu•at•ed, fluc•tu•at•ing, fluc•tu•ates.** to change in unexpected or unpredictable ways. *The water temperature of the pool seemed to fluctuate daily.* —**fluc•tu•a•tion** *n.*

flu•ent /flo͞o′ ənt/ *adj.* able to speak smoothly and easily. *She was fluent in both French and English.* —**flu•ent•ly** *adv.* —**flu•en•cy** *n.*

for•mal[1] /fôr′ məl/ *adj.* done in a proper or ceremonious manner. *A formal meeting was held by the group.* —**for•mal•ly** *adv.*

for•mal[2] /fôr′ məl/ *n.* a social affair or the type of dress required for a social affair. *Jane bought a new formal for the dance.*

for•te[1] /fôr′ tā′ *or* fôrt/ *n.* something that one does very well; a specialty. *The teacher's forte is math.*

for•te[2] /fôr′ tā′/ *adv.* loudly and forcefully. *The orchestra played the music forte.*

frac•ture[1] /frăk′ chər/ *n.* a break or crack. *The football player had a leg fracture.*

frac•ture[2] /frăk′ chər/ *v.* **frac•tured, frac•tur•ing, frac•tures.** to break or crack. *The vase fractured when it hit the floor.*

G

gen•der /jĕn′ dər/ *n.* the classification or category of male or female. *Applications for work no longer require that we specify gender.*

ge•ne•al•o•gy /jē′ nē ŏl′ ə jē *or* jē′ nē ăl′ ə jē/ *n., pl.* **ge•ne•al•o•gies.** family history. *My grandmother has traced our family's genealogy back to the Revolutionary War.* —**ge•ne•a•log•i•cal** *adj.* —**ge•ne•a•log•i•cal•ly** *adv.* —**ge•ne•al•o•gist** *n.*

gen•er•a•tion[1] /jĕn′ ə rā′ shən/ *n.* people born about the same time. *This generation of children is skilled at using computers.* —**gen•er•a•tion•al** *adj.*

gen•er•a•tion[2] /jĕn′ ə rā′ shən/ *n.* the length of time between the birth of parents and the birth of their children. *My family has owned this house for three generations.* —**gen•er•a•tion•al** *adj.*

gen•er•a•tion[3] /jĕn′ ə rā′ shən/ *n.* the development and improvement of objects so as to create a new and distinct class. *A new generation of computers has changed our way of storing written material.* —**gen•er•a•tion•al** *adj.*

gen•er•os•i•ty /jĕn′ ə rŏs′ ĭ tē/ *n., pl.* **gen•er•os•i•ties.** the willingness to give or share. *We appreciated his generosity in supporting our school.*

gen•er•ous /jĕn′ ər əs/ *adj.* giving freely; unselfish. *John has always been generous with his time.* —**gen•er•ous•ly** *adv.* —**gen•er•ous•ness** *n.*

glo•ri•ous[1] /glôr′ ē əs *or* glōr′ ē əs/ *adj.* deserving of or bringing great honor. *The glorious victory was celebrated for days.* —**glo•ri•ous•ly** *adv.* —**glo•ri•ous•ness** *n.*

glo•ri•ous[2] /glôr′ ē əs *or* glōr′ ē əs/ *adj.* beautiful; magnificent. *We watched the glorious sunset.* —**glo•ri•ous•ly** *adv.* —**glo•ri•ous•ness** *n.*

PRONUNCIATION KEY

/ă/	pat
/ā/	pay
/â/	care
/ä/	father
/är/	far
/ĕ/	pet
/ē/	be
/ĭ/	pit
/ī/	pie
/îr/	pier
/ŏ/	mop
/ō/	toe
/ô/	paw, for
/oi/	noise
/ou/	out
/ŏŏ/	look
/ōō/	boot
/ŭ/	cut
/ûr/	urge
/th/	thin
/th/	this
/hw/	what
/zh/	vision
/ə/	about
	item
	pencil
	gallop
	circus
/ər/	butter

glo•ry[1] /glôr′ ē or glōr′ ē/ *n., pl.* **glo•ries.** honor; fame; high achievement. *The heroic act won her glory.*

glo•ry[2] /glôr′ ē or glōr′ ē/ *n., pl.* **glo•ries.** beauty. *Everyone noticed the flowers' glory.*

glo•ry[3] /glôr′ ē or glōr′ ē/ *v.* **glo•ried, glo•ry•ing, glo•ries.** to be happy about something. *Parents glory in their children's achievements.*

grad•u•al /grăj′ ōō əl/ *adj.* happening little by little. *The gradual rise in temperature was hardly noticed.* —**grad•u•al•ly** *adv.* —**grad•u•al•ness** *n.*

grad•u•ate[1] /grăj′ ōō āt′/ *v.* **grad•u•at•ed, grad•u•at•ing, grad•u•ates.** to earn a degree or diploma. *He will graduate from high school next year.*

grad•u•ate[2] /grăj′ ōō āt′/ *v.* **grad•u•at•ed, grad•u•at•ing, grad•u•ates.** to mark intervals in order to measure. *A ruler is graduated in inches.*

grad•u•ate[3] /grăj′ ōō ĭt/ *n.* a person who has earned a diploma. *My sister is a graduate of Springfield High School.*

grave[1] /grāv/ *n.* a place of burial. *We found a very old grave in the cemetery.*

grave[2] /grāv/ *adj.* **grav•er, grav•est.** serious; very important. *We had a grave decision to make.* —**grave•ly** *adv.* —**grave•ness** *n.*

grave[3] /grāv/ *adj.* **grav•er, grav•est.** dangerous; very harmful. *The doctor said his condition was grave.* —**grave•ly** *adv.* —**grave•ness** *n.*

grave[4] /grāv/ *adj.* **grav•er, grav•est.** somber. *My father's grave expression indicated the news was not good.* —**grave•ly** *adv.* —**grave•ness** *n.*

grav•i•tate /grăv′ ĭ tāt′/ *v.* **grav•i•tat•ed, grav•i•tat•ing, grav•i•tates.** to move because of gravity; to move downward. *Water gravitates to the lowest possible area.*

grief /grēf/ *n.* sorrow; suffering. *His grief showed through his tears.*

griev•ous /grē′ vəs/ *adj.* causing great sorrow or suffering; serious. *To accuse him unfairly is a grievous injustice.* —**griev•ous•ly** *adv.* —**griev•ous•ness** *n.*

grudge[1] /grŭj/ *v.* **grudged, grudg•ing, grudg•es.** to give unwillingly. *The selfish man grudged only a small amount of help.* —**grudg•ing•ly** *adv.* —**grudg•er** *n.*

grudge[2] /grŭj/ *n.* a feeling of hostility toward another; resentment. *I try not to hold a grudge when someone else wins.*

grudg•ing /grŭj′ ĭng/ *adj.* unwilling. *He admitted his guilt in a grudging manner.* —**grudg•ing•ly** *adv.*

har•mo•ny[1] /här′ mə nē/ *n., pl.* **har•mo•nies.** agreement; friendliness. *Good manners help maintain harmony in our classroom.*

har•mo•ny[2] /här′ mə nē/ *n., pl.* **har•mo•nies.** a combination of musical notes that are pleasant to hear. *The song has a nice harmony.*

heir[1] /âr/ *n.* a person who has received or will receive property or a title belonging to another. *The old man's heir was listed in his will.*

heir[2] /âr/ *n.* a person who receives ideas from someone who lived earlier. *We are the lucky heirs of many early inventions.*

he•red•i•ty /hə rĕd′ ĭ tē/ *n., pl.* **he•red•i•ties.** the transmission or passing of traits or physical characteristics from parents to children. *Heredity has caused many in my family to have red hair.*

hos•pi•tal•i•ty /hŏs′ pĭ tăl′ ĭ tē/ *n., pl.* **hos•pi•tal•i•ties.** the act of showing kindness and warmth toward guests. *Her hospitality made us feel welcome.*

hu•mane /hyōō mān′/ *adj.* kind or compassionate to people or animals. *Our country believes we should treat prisoners in a humane way.* —**hu•mane•ly** *adv.* —**hu•mane•ness** *n.*

hy•drau•lics /hī drô′ lĭks/ *n. (used with a singular verb)* the science involving the study of liquids. *We observed principles of hydraulics when we visited the waterfall.*

hy•dro•e•lec•tric /hī′ drō ĭ lĕk′ trĭk/ *adj.* related to the production of electricity from the energy of running water. *A hydroelectric plant produces electricity for our city.* —**hy•dro•e•lec•tri•cal•ly** *adv.*

hy•dro•gen /hī′ drə jən/ *n. Symbol* **H**. a colorless, odorless, but highly flammable gas found throughout the universe. *Scientists take great care when using hydrogen.*

hy•dro•pho•bi•a[1] /hī′ drə fō′ bē ə/ *n.* an extreme fear of water. *Hydrophobia keeps some people from enjoying swimming.*

hy•dro•pho•bi•a[2] /hī′ drə fō′ bē ə/ *n.* the disease known as rabies. *Vaccinations are required for dogs to prevent hydrophobia.*

I

il•lus•tri•ous /ĭ lŭs′ trē əs/ *adj.* well known; famous. *The illustrious author was asked to speak at the dinner.*

im•mi•nent /ĭm′ ə nənt/ *adj.* coming soon; ready to happen. *His arrival is imminent.* —**im•mi•nent•ly** *adv.* —**im•mi•nence** *n.* —**im•mi•nent•ness** *n.*

im•mod•est[1] /ĭ mŏd′ ĭst/ *adj.* tending to praise oneself. *It was immodest of you to tell everyone about your high score.* —**im•mod•est•ly** *adv.* —**im•mod•es•ty** *n.*

im•mod•est[2] /ĭ mŏd′ ĭst/ *adj.* indecent; improper. *Our school does not allow students to wear immodest clothing.* —**im•mod•est•ly** *adv.* —**im•mod•es•ty** *n.*

im•pede /ĭm pēd′/ *v.* **im•ped•ed, im•ped•ing, im•pedes.** to interfere with the progress of; to block. *Construction work impeded the flow of traffic.*

im•pend /ĭm pĕnd′/ *v.* **im•pend•ed, im•pend•ing, im•pends.** to be about to happen; to threaten. *A thunderstorm impends.*

im•pend•ing /ĭm pĕnd′ ĭng/ *adj.* about to happen. *The impending rain may cause our game to be canceled.*

im•per•ti•nent[1] /ĭm pûr′ tn ənt/ *adj.* rude; insolent. *The child's impertinent behavior annoyed everyone.* —**im•per•ti•nent•ly** *adv.*

im•per•ti•nent[2] /ĭm pûr′ tn ənt/ *adj.* not pertaining to; unrelated. *The message was impertinent to our job.* —**im•per•ti•nent•ly** *adv.*

im•pul•sive /ĭm pŭl′ sĭv/ *adj.* acting without thought. *My impulsive remark angered my friend.* —**im•pul•sive•ly** *adv.* —**im•pul•sive•ness** *n.*

in•can•des•cent /ĭn′ kən dĕs′ ənt/ *adj.* very bright with intense heat. *The sun is a source of incandescent light.* —**in•can•des•cent•ly** *adv.* —**in•can•des•cence** *n.*

in•ca•pa•ble /ĭn kā′ pə bəl/ *adj.* lacking ability or strength. *We were incapable of hiking another mile.* —**in•ca•pa•bil•i•ty** *n.*

in•dig•nant /ĭn dĭg′ nənt/ *adj.* feeling anger over injustice or unfairness. *The customer was indignant about having to wait so long.* —**in•dig•nant•ly** *adv.*

in•flam•ma•tion /ĭn′ flə mā′ shən/ *n.* a redness and swelling in reaction to infection or injury. *An ice pack helped reduce the inflammation of her sprained ankle.*

in•flict /ĭn flĭkt′/ *v.* **in•flict•ed, in•flict•ing, in•flicts.** to cause. *The storm inflicted damage in the community.*

in•for•mal /ĭn fôr′ məl/ *adj.* without ceremony; not formal. *We had an informal gathering to celebrate Sam's birthday.* —**in•for•mal•ly** *adv.*

in•her•it[1] /ĭn hĕr′ ĭt/ *v.* **in•her•it•ed, in•her•it•ing, in•her•its.** to receive money, property, or a title from an ancestor. *I inherited some money for college from my grandmother.* —**in•her•i•tor** *n.*

in•her•it[2] /ĭn hĕr′ ĭt/ *v.* **in•her•it•ed, in•her•it•ing, in•her•its.** to acquire traits or physical characteristics from one's parents. *I inherited my mother's musical ability.* —**in•her•i•tor** *n.*

in•her•it[3] /ĭn hĕr′ ĭt/ *v.* **in•her•it•ed, in•her•it•ing, in•her•its.** to take over something. *Whoever becomes president will inherit many unfinished tasks.* —**in•her•i•tor** *n.*

in•her•i•tance[1] /ĭn hĕr′ ĭ təns/ *n.* the physical characteristics and traits passed on to one's children. *My blue eyes are an inheritance from my father.*

in•her•i•tance² /ĭn hĕr' ĭ təns/ *n.* the money, property, or title which has been or will be inherited. *Amy saved her inheritance for college.*

in•her•i•tance³ /ĭn hĕr' ĭ təns/ *n.* tradition; heritage. *Freedom of speech is part of our national inheritance.*

in•i•ti•ate¹ /ĭ nĭsh' ē āt/ *v.* **in•i•ti•at•ed, in•i•ti•at•ing, in•i•ti•ates.** to begin. *We initiated the program by singing our school song.* —**in•i•ti•a•tor** *n.*

in•i•ti•ate² /ĭ nĭsh' ē āt/ *v.* **in•i•ti•at•ed, in•i•ti•at•ing, in•i•ti•ates.** to bring a new person into a group. *A special ceremony initiated the new members.* —**in•i•ti•a•tor** *n.*

in•quire /ĭn kwīr'/ *v.* **in•quired, in•quir•ing, in•quires.** to try to find information. *Jane inquired about the school's athletic policy.* —**in•quir•ing•ly** *adv.* —**in•quir•er** *n.*

in•ter /ĭn tûr'/ *v.* **in•terred, in•ter•ring, in•ters.** to bury. *The body was interred in the cemetery.*

in•ter•act /ĭn' tər ăkt'/ *v.* **in•ter•act•ed, in•ter•act•ing, in•ter•acts.** to act upon or with one another. *The children interacted on the playground.* —**in•ter•ac•tive** *adj.*

in•ter•ac•tion /ĭn' tər ăk' shən/ *n.* the result of things acting upon or with one another. *Our interaction at lunch was pleasant.*

in•ter•im¹ /ĭn' tər ĭm/ *n.* the time between events. *There was a thirty-minute interim between the games.*

in•ter•im² /ĭn' tər ĭm/ *adj.* temporary. *The interim principal will be here the rest of the year.*

in•va•lid¹ /ĭn' və lĭd/ *n.* a person unable to function without help. *The nurse helped the invalid into a wheelchair.*

in•val•id² /ĭn văl' ĭd/ *adj.* not legal or proper. *Her driver's license will be invalid if she doesn't renew it.* —**in•val•id•ly** *adv.* —**in•va•lid•i•ty** *n.*

in•vo•ca•tion /ĭn' və kā' shən/ *n.* a calling upon for help or protection. *Many volunteers answered the invocation and joined the charity.*

in•voke¹ /ĭn vōk'/ *v.* **in•voked, in•vok•ing, in•vokes.** to call upon for help or protection. *The small town invoked help from the military.*

in•voke² /ĭn vōk'/ *v.* **in•voked, in•vok•ing, in•vokes.** to make use of or to apply a rule. *The president has the authority to invoke his veto power.*

kiln /kĭln *or* kĭl/ *n.* a furnace for melting glass or drying clay. *We watched as the vase was heated in the kiln.*

L

league¹ /lēg/ *n.* an association of people who have a common interest. *Women interested in political issues have formed a league.*

league² /lēg/ *n.* sports teams who compete against one another. *Our high school joined a new football league.*

liq•ue•fy *or* **liq•ui•fy** /lĭk' wə fī/ *v.* **liq•ue•fied, liq•ue•fy•ing, liq•ue•fies.** to make liquid. *A very high temperature will liquefy the metal.* —**liq•ue•fi•a•ble** *adj.* —**liq•ue•fi•er** *n.*

lu•cent /lōō' sənt/ *adj.* giving off light. *The lucent moon shone brightly in the sky.* —**lu•cent•ly** *adv.* —**lu•cen•cy** *n.*

lu•cid¹ /lōō' sĭd/ *adj.* easily understood. *Her lucid explanation cleared up the confusion.* —**lu•cid•ly** *adv.* —**lu•cid•i•ty** *n.* —**lu•cid•ness** *n.*

lu•cid² /lōō' sĭd/ *adj.* mentally aware. *The patient's lucid answers showed his recovery was complete.* —**lu•cid•ly** *adv.* —**lu•cid•i•ty** *n.* —**lu•cid•ness** *n.*

lu•mi•nar•y¹ /lōō' mə nĕr' ē/ *n., pl.* **lu•mi•nar•ies.** a person who is well known; a high-achieving person. *The presence of a luminary drew many people to the ceremony.*

lu•mi•nar•y² /lōō' mə nĕr' ē/ *n., pl.* **lu•mi•nar•ies.** a heavenly body that gives off light. *The Milky Way is made up of millions of luminaries.*

lu•mi•nes•cent /lōō′ mə **nĕs′** ənt/ *adj.* giving out light without much heat. *Fluorescent bulbs produce luminescent light.* —**lu•mi•nes•cence** *n.*

lu•mi•nous¹ /lōō′ mə nəs/ *adj.* having its own light; bright. *The stars are luminous.* —**lu•mi•nous•ly** *adv.* —**lu•mi•nous•ness.** *n.*

lu•mi•nous² /lōō′ mə nəs/ *adj.* can be understood; clear. *The luminous directions made the work easy.* —**lu•mi•nous•ly** *adv.* —**lu•mi•nous•ness.** *n.*

lus•ter¹ /lŭs′ tər/ *n.* gloss; sheen; brightness. *The wax gave our car a shiny luster.*

lus•ter² /lŭs′ tər/ *n.* greatness or glory. *The talented singer's luster was noted in the magazine.*

ma•nip•u•late¹ /mə nĭp′ yə lāt′/ *v.* **ma•nip•u•lat•ed, ma•nip•u•lat•ing, ma•nip•u•lates.** to work or handle skillfully. *It took great skill to manipulate the objects into place.* —**ma•nip•u•la•tive** *adj.* —**ma•nip•u•la•tor** *n.*

ma•nip•u•late² /mə nĭp′ yə lāt′/ *v.* **ma•nip•u•lat•ed, ma•nip•u•lat•ing, ma•nip•u•lates.** to influence others indirectly. *We did not realize that his flattery was an attempt to manipulate us.* —**ma•nip•u•la•tive** *adj.* —**ma•nip•u•la•tor** *n.*

mar•shal¹ /mär′ shəl/ *v.* **mar•shaled, mar•shal•ing, mar•shals** or **mar•shalled, mar•shal•ling, mar•shals.** to organize or place in an orderly way. *We marshaled our efforts in order to make the work easier.*

mar•shal² /mär′ shəl/ *n.* a person in charge; a person in a high position. *She was honored to be the parade marshal.*

ma•ture¹ /mə tyŏŏr′ *or* mə tŏŏr′ *or* mə chŏŏr′/ *adj.* **ma•tur•er, ma•tur•est.** fully grown or developed. *The mature apples will be picked this week.* —**ma•ture•ly** *adv.* —**ma•ture•ness** *n.* —**ma•tu•ri•ty** *n.*

ma•ture² /mə tyŏŏr′ *or* mə tŏŏr′ *or* mə chŏŏr′/ *adj.* **ma•tur•er, ma•tur•est.** showing qualities of full physical and mental development. *The movie is for mature audiences.* —**ma•ture•ly** *adv.* —**ma•ture•ness** *n.* —**ma•tu•ri•ty** *n.*

ma•ture³ /mə tyŏŏr′ *or* mə tŏŏr′ *or* mə chŏŏr′/ *v.* **ma•tured, ma•tur•ing, ma•tures.** to complete growth. *Some animals mature in a very short time.*

men•ace¹ /mĕn′ ĭs/ *n.* something that can cause injury or harm; a threat or hazard. *Objects left on stairs are a menace.*

men•ace² /mĕn′ ĭs/ *v.* **men•aced, men•ac•ing, men•ac•es.** to threaten. *The bully menaced the young children.* —**men•ac•ing•ly** *adv.* —**men•ac•er** *n.*

mi•crobes /mī′ krōbs′/ *n.* minute organisms. *Disease-causing microbes often cannot be seen without a microscope.* —**mi•cro•bi•al** /mī krō′ bē əl/ *adj.*

mol•e•cule /mŏl′ ĭ kyōōl′/ *n.* a small unit made up of two or more atoms; the basis of all substances. *Scientists study molecules to learn how substances are formed.*

mol•ten /mōl′ tən/ *adj.* melted by heat. *Molten iron is used to make steel.*

mon•o•chro•mat•ic /mŏn′ ə krō mătʹ ĭk/ *adj.* made up of one color. *The room was decorated in a monochromatic color scheme.* —**mon•o•chro•mat•i•cal•ly** *adv.*

mute¹ /myōōt/ *v.* **mut•ed, mut•ing, mutes.** to muffle or lessen sound. *He uses a special attachment to mute the sound of his trumpet.* —**mute•ly** *adv.* —**mute•ness** *n.*

mute² /myōōt/ *adj.* unable to speak. *The mute child communicated through signing.* —**mute•ly** *adv.* —**mute•ness** *n.*

nau•se•a /nô′ zē ə *or* nô′ zhə/ *n.* a sick feeling; the need to vomit. *His nausea went away when he got off of the ship.*

nau•ti•cal /nô′ tĭ kəl/ *adj.* having to do with water, ships, or navigation. *The ship's captain measured distance in nautical miles.* —**nau•ti•cal•ly** *adv.*

non•de•script /nŏn′ dĭ **skrĭpt′**/ *adj.* having no distinctive qualities. *The outside of the building was nondescript.*

no•to•ri•ous /nō tôr′ ē əs *or* nō tōr′ ē əs/ *adj.* well-known in an unfavorable manner; infamous. *Jesse James was a notorious outlaw.* —**no•to•ri•ous•ly** *adv.* —**no•to•ri•ous•ness** *n.*

nui•sance /nōō′ səns *or* nyōō′ səns/ *n.* something that annoys; an inconvenience. *The long wait was a nuisance when we needed to hurry.*

O

ob•li•gate /ŏb′ lĭ gāt′/ *v.* **ob•li•gat•ed, ob•li•gat•ing, ob•li•gates.** to demand or compel as a moral or legal responsibility. *Citizenship obligates one to vote.* —**ob•li•ga•tor** *n.*

ob•li•ga•tion /ŏb′ lĭ gā′ shən/ *n.* a responsibility; a sense of duty. *Tommy's obligation was completed when he finished the report.*

o•blige¹ /ə blīj′/ *v.* **o•bliged, o•blig•ing, o•blig•es.** to require. *I am obliged to return my library books.*

o•blige² /ə blīj′/ *v.* **o•bliged, o•blig•ing, o•blig•es.** to make thankful, grateful, or indebted. *My father was obliged for the help he was given.*

ob•sess /əb sĕs′ *or* ŏb sĕs′/ *v.* **ob•sessed, ob•sess•ing, ob•sess•es.** to be in one's mind more than normal. *Jill was obsessed with electronic games.*

ob•ses•sion /əb sĕsh′ ən *or* ŏb sĕsh′ ən/ *n.* an idea or desire that keeps coming into the mind. *Andrew's obsession with sports interfered with his studying.* —**ob•ses•sion•al** *adj.*

ob•ses•sive /əb sĕs′ ĭv *or* ŏb sĕs′ ĭv/ *adj.* relating to an idea or desire that keeps coming into the mind. *Her obsessive personality affected everything she did.*

ob•sti•na•cy /ŏb′ stə nə sē/ *n.* the state or quality of being stubborn. *Obstinacy is a difficult quality to deal with in a friend.*

ob•sti•nate /ŏb′ stə nĭt/ *adj.* unwilling to change; stubborn. *My obstinate friend refused to use the new computer.* —**ob•sti•nate•ly** *adv.* —**ob•sti•nate•ness** *n.*

oc•ca•sion /ə kā′ zhən/ *n.* a special event. *A birthday is an exciting occasion.*

oc•ca•sion•al¹ /ə kā′ zhə nəl/ *adj.* happening from time to time. *We heard an occasional whisper.* —**oc•ca•sion•al•ly** *adv.*

oc•ca•sion•al² /ə kā′ zhə nəl/ *adj.* for special use or need. *A piece of occasional music was played at the wedding.*

oc•cur¹ /ə kûr′/ *v.* **oc•curred, oc•cur•ring, oc•curs.** to take place. *The event will occur this afternoon.*

oc•cur² /ə kûr′/ *v.* **oc•curred, oc•cur•ring, oc•curs.** to come to mind. *It occurred to me that you might need the book.*

oc•cur•rence /ə kûr′ əns/ *n.* something that takes place; a happening. *Her birthday party was a happy occurrence.*

op•press /ə prĕs′/ *v.* **op•pressed, op•press•ing, op•press•es.** to keep down by using unfair treatment; to treat harshly. *Some governments oppress people.* —**op•pres•sor** *n.*

op•pres•sive /ə prĕs′ ĭv/ *adj.* difficult to bear; burdensome. *Years of oppressive treatment will lead to a revolution.*

op•ti•mism /ŏp′ tə mĭz′ əm/ *n.* a positive attitude; confidence that good will happen. *His optimism encouraged us to continue.*

op•ti•mis•tic /ŏp′ tə mĭs′ tĭk/ *adj.* hopeful; expecting a good outcome. *Amy is an optimistic person.* —**op•ti•mis•ti•cal•ly** *adv.*

o•ra•tion /ô rā′ shən/ *n.* a formal speech on a special occasion. *Nancy was asked to give an oration at the graduation program.*

o•ri•ent¹ /ôr′ ē ĕnt′/ *v.* **o•ri•ent•ed, o•ri•ent•ing, o•ri•ents.** to place according to compass points. *The builder wanted to orient the house to face north.*

o•ri•ent² /ôr′ ē ĕnt′/ *v.* **o•ri•ent•ed, o•ri•ent•ing, o•ri•ents.** to make familiar. *We can help to orient the new student to our school.*

PRONUNCIATION KEY	
/ă/	pat
/ā/	pay
/â/	care
/ä/	father
/är/	far
/ĕ/	pet
/ē/	be
/ĭ/	pit
/ī/	pie
/îr/	pier
/ŏ/	mop
/ō/	toe
/ô/	paw, for
/oi/	noise
/ou/	out
/ŏŏ/	look
/ōō/	boot
/ŭ/	cut
/ûr/	urge
/th/	thin
/th/	this
/hw/	what
/zh/	vision
/ə/	about
	item
	pencil
	gallop
	circus
/ər/	butter

o•ri•en•ta•tion¹ /ôr′ ē ən tā′ shən/ *n.* knowing where you are in relation to your surroundings. *A map is very helpful in getting your orientation in a strange city.*

o•ri•en•ta•tion² /ôr′ ē ən tā′ shən/ *n.* instruction to develop awareness of something new. *The school offers an orientation to new students.*

or•i•gin¹ /ôr′ ə jĭn *or* ŏr′ ə jĭn/ *n.* the source. *The origin of that folktale is a mystery.*

or•i•gin² /ôr′ ə jĭn *or* ŏr′ ə jĭn/ *n.* having to do with ancestry. *My father's family is of German origin.*

o•rig•i•nal¹ /ə rĭj′ ə nəl/ *adj.* first. *I made copies of the original document.*

o•rig•i•nal² /ə rĭj′ ə nəl/ *adj.* able to produce new ideas or ways of doing something. *Brad is an original thinker and often comes up with new ideas.*

or•nate /ôr nāt′/ *adj.* richly or extravagantly decorated. *The king wore an ornate crown.* —**or•nate•ly** *adv.* —**or•nate•ness** *n.*

par•a•lyze /păr′ ə līz′/ *v.* **par•a•lyzed, par•a•lyz•ing, par•a•lyz•es.** to make unable to move. *A back injury paralyzed her.* —**par•a•ly•za•tion** /păr′ ə lĭ zā′ shən/ *n.* —**par•a•lyz•er** *n.*

per•sist¹ /pər sĭst′/ *v.* **per•sist•ed, per•sist•ing, per•sists.** to keep trying; to insist. *She persisted in trying to play the piano.*

per•sist² /pər sĭst′/ *v.* **per•sist•ed, per•sist•ing, per•sists.** to last; to continue. *The heat will persist for several weeks.*

per•sist•ent¹ /pər sĭs′ tənt/ *adj.* lasting; continuous. *His persistent cough worried his mother.* —**per•sist•ent•ly** *adv.*

per•sist•ent² /pər sĭs′ tənt/ *adj.* not giving up. *Joe's persistent effort brought good results.* —**per•sist•ent•ly** *adv.*

per•spire /pər spīr′/ *v.* **per•spired, per•spir•ing, per•spires.** to sweat. *Your body perspires to stay cool.* —**per•spi•ra•tion** *n.*

per•sua•sive /pər swā′ sĭv/ *adj.* having the power to change someone's thinking. *I voted for Amy after listening to her persuasive speech.* —**per•sua•sive•ly** *adv.* —**per•sua•sive•ness** *n.*

pes•ky /pĕs′ kē/ *adj.* **pes•ki•er, pes•ki•est.** annoying; bothersome. *The pesky squirrel would not stay away from our bird feeder.* —**pes•ki•ly** *adv.* —**pes•ki•ness** *n.*

pet•ri•fied /pĕt′ rə fīd′/ *adj.* stone-like. *Petrified wood is a type of fossil.*

pet•ri•fy¹ /pĕt′ rə fī′/ *v.* **pet•ri•fied, pet•ri•fy•ing, pet•ri•fies.** to turn into stone or a stone-like substance. *Ordinary processes of nature petrified the wood.*

pet•ri•fy² /pĕt′ rə fī′/ *v.* **pet•ri•fied, pet•ri•fy•ing, pet•ri•fies.** to paralyze or stun with terror. *The large dog petrified the child.*

pe•tro•le•um /pə trō′ lē əm/ *n.* a thick, flammable liquid usually found beneath the earth's surface. *Offshore drilling has increased our supply of petroleum.*

phys•i•cal¹ /fĭz′ ə kəl/ *adj.* having to do with the body. *Exercise helps maintain physical strength.* —**phys•i•cal•ly** *adv.*

phys•i•cal² /fĭz′ ə kəl/ *adj.* relating to nature or nonliving matter. *By studying a physical map, we located all of Asia's mountains.* —**phys•i•cal•ly** *adv.*

phys•i•cal³ /fĭz′ ə kəl/ *n.* an examination by a doctor to determine health. *A physical was required before I could participate in soccer.*

phys•i•ol•o•gy /fĭz′ ē ŏl′ ə jē/ *n.* the study of the functions and vital processes of living organisms. *He learned how the body functions through classes in physiology.* —**phys•i•ol•o•gist** *n.*

pin•cers¹ /pĭn′ sərz/ *pl. n.* (used with a singular or plural verb) a gripping and flattening tool made of two hinged parts. *We used pincers to hold the parts in place.*

pin•cers² /pĭn′ sərz/ *pl. n.* (used with a singular or plural verb) a grasping claw used for holding. *The lobster used its pincers as a tool.*

plac•id /plăs′ ĭd/ *adj.* calm; peaceful. *She is a very placid child.* —**plac•id•ly** *adv.* —**pla•cid•i•ty** *n.* —**plac•id•ness** *n.*

pli•a•ble[1] /plī′ ə bəl/ *n.* shaped or bent easily; flexible. *We used pliable wire to hang the decoration.* —**pli•a•bly** *adv.* —**pli•a•bil•i•ty** *n.* —**pli•a•ble•ness** *n.*

pli•a•ble[2] /plī′ ə bəl/ *adj.* easily persuaded. *We can convince those with pliable minds.* —**pli•a•bly** *adv.* —**pli•a•bil•i•ty** *n.* —**pli•a•ble•ness** *n.*

ply[1] /plī/ *n., pl.* **plies** /plīz/. thickness or layer. *The extra ply in this rope makes it stronger.*

ply[2] /plī/ *v.* **plied** /plīd/, **ply•ing, plies** /plīz/. to use as a tool. *Early settlers quickly learned to ply an axe.*

post•pone /pōst pōn′ *or* pŏs pōn′/ *v.* **post•poned, post•pon•ing, post•pones.** to put off until a later time. *I will postpone the appointment.* —**post•pon•a•ble** *adj.* —**post•pone•ment** *n.* —**post•pon•er** *n.*

pos•ture[1] /pŏs′ chər/ *n.* how a person holds or carries his or her body. *Physical exercise helps maintain good posture.*

pos•ture[2] /pŏs′ chər/ *v.* **pos•tured, pos•tur•ing, pos•tures.** to assume a pose or an attitude for effect. *The actor postured in front of the audience.*

po•tent /pōt′ nt/ *adj.* powerful; highly effective. *The doctor said that the medicine was very potent.* —**po•tent•ly** *adv.* —**po•tent•ness** *n.*

pre•cede /prĭ sēd′/ *v.* **pre•ced•ed, pre•ced•ing, pre•cedes.** to come before in time or order. *High school precedes college.*

pre•cur•sor /prĭ kûr′ sər *or* prē′ kûr′ sər/ *n.* a forerunner; something that comes before something else. *Kindergarten is a precursor to first grade.*

pre•de•ter•mine[1] /prē′ dĭ tûr′ mĭn/ *v.* **pre•de•ter•mined, pre•de•ter•min•ing, pre•de•ter•mines.** to decide in advance. *We can predetermine the time that we'll need for the project.* —**pre•de•ter•mi•na•tion** *n.* —**pre•de•ter•min•er** *n.*

pre•de•ter•mine[2] /prē′ dĭ tûr′ mĭn/ *v.* **pre•de•ter•mined, pre•de•ter•min•ing, pre•de•ter•mines.** to influence others. *The outcome of the vote was predetermined by the candidate's excellent campaign.* —**pre•de•ter•mi•na•tion** *n.* —**pre•de•ter•min•er** *n.*

pre•ma•ture /prē′ mə tyoŏr′ *or* prē′ mə toŏr′ *or* prē′ mə choŏr′/ *adj.* before expected; too early. *Tommy's premature arrival spoiled the surprise.* —**pre•ma•ture•ly** *adv.* —**pre•ma•ture•ness** *n.* —**pre•ma•tu•ri•ty** *n.*

pre•ten•tious[1] /prĭ tĕn′ shəs/ *adj.* claiming certain merit or position. *His pretentious remarks did not impress his boss.* —**pre•ten•tious•ly** *adv.* —**pre•ten•tious•ness** *n.*

pre•ten•tious[2] /prĭ tĕn′ shəs/ *adj.* extravagant; showy. *Her pretentious home led us to believe she was wealthy.* —**pre•ten•tious•ly** *adv.* —**pre•ten•tious•ness** *n.*

pro•ceed /prō sēd′ *or* prə sēd′/ *v.* **pro•ceed•ed, pro•ceed•ing, pro•ceeds.** to go forward; to go on. *The game will proceed when the buzzer sounds.*

prog•e•ny /prŏj′ ə nē/ *n., pl.* **progeny** *or* **prog•e•nies.** children; descendants. *We challenge our progeny to create a safer world.*

prog•ress[1] /prŏg′ rĕs′ *or* prō′ grĕs′/ *n.* advancement; improvement. *Scientists have made progress in computer technology.*

pro•gress[2] /prə grĕs′/ *v.* **pro•gressed, pro•gress•ing, pro•gress•es.** to improve or advance. *His basketball skills progressed a lot this year.*

prov•o•ca•tion /prŏv′ ə kā′ shən/ *n.* something that causes anger or strong feeling. *An insult was the last provocation before the fight broke out.*

pro•voc•a•tive /prə vŏk′ ə tĭv/ *adj.* tending to cause anger or strong feeling. *Many political issues tend to be very provocative.*

PRONUNCIATION KEY	
/ă/	pat
/ā/	pay
/â/	care
/ä/	father
/är/	far
/ĕ/	pet
/ē/	be
/ĭ/	pit
/ī/	pie
/îr/	pier
/ŏ/	mop
/ō/	toe
/ô/	paw, for
/oi/	noise
/ou/	out
/oŏ/	look
/oō/	boot
/ŭ/	cut
/ûr/	urge
/th/	thin
/th/	this
/hw/	what
/zh/	vision
/ə/	about
	item
	pencil
	gallop
	circus
/ər/	butter

pro•voke /prə vōk′/ v. **pro•voked, pro•vok•ing, pro•vokes.** to cause anger or strong feeling. *The student's behavior provoked the bus driver.* —**pro•vok•ing•ly** adv.

R

rap•port /ră pôr′ or rə pôr′/ n. a friendly, trusting relationship. *I have a wonderful rapport with my cousin.*

re•cep•tive /rĭ sĕp′ tĭv/ adj. willing to accept; agreeable. *Our principal is receptive to new ideas.* —**re•cep•tive•ly** adv. —**re•cep•tive•ness** n.

re•cur[1] /rĭ kûr′/ v. **re•curred, re•cur•ring, re•curs.** to happen again; to repeat. *We didn't expect the error to recur.* —**re•cur•rence** n.

re•cur[2] /rĭ kûr′/ v. **re•curred, re•cur•ring, re•curs.** to return in thought or memory. *I finally tried the idea that kept recurring in my mind.* —**re•cur•rence** n.

re•cur•rent /rĭ kûr′ ənt or rĭ kŭr′ ənt/ adj. repeated; occurring regularly. *The recurrent announcement reminded us to use caution.* —**re•cur•rent•ly** adv. —**re•cur•rence** n.

re•flect[1] /rĭ flĕkt′/ v. **re•flect•ed, re•flect•ing, re•flects.** to bend or cause to go in a different direction, such as light rays. *A mirror can reflect light.*

re•flect[2] /rĭ flĕkt′/ v. **re•flect•ed, re•flect•ing, re•flects.** to mirror an image. *The still water in the lake reflected the mountain.*

re•flect[3] /rĭ flĕkt′/ v. **re•flect•ed, re•flect•ing, re•flects.** to represent. *Gasoline prices often reflect the amount of oil available.*

re•flex /rē′ flĕks′/ n., pl. **re•flex•es.** a response made without thought; an involuntary response. *The doctor taps my knee to check my reflex.*

re•frain[1] /rĭ frān′/ n. a repeated phrase. *Everyone joined in when the choir sang the refrain.*

re•frain[2] /rĭ frān′/ v. **re•frained, re•frain•ing, re•frains.** to avoid doing something. *I will refrain from talking during the movie.*

re•gress /rĭ grĕs′/ v. **re•gressed, re•gress•ing, re•gress•es.** to move to a prior position; to move backward. *I regressed in my exercise program during the winter.* —**re•gres•sor** n.

re•ju•ve•nate /rĭ jōō′ və nāt′/ v. **re•ju•ve•nat•ed, re•ju•ve•nat•ing, re•ju•ve•nates.** to make strong again. *We were very tired, but a good night's sleep rejuvenated us.* —**re•ju•ve•na•tion** n. —**re•ju•ve•na•tor** n.

rel•e•vant /rĕl′ ə vənt/ adj. connected or related to something. *His story was relevant to our conversation.* —**rel•e•vant•ly** adv. —**rel•e•vance** n. —**rel•e•van•cy** n.

re•lin•quish /rĭ lĭng′ kwĭsh/ v. **re•lin•quished, re•lin•quish•ing, re•lin•quish•es.** to give up something; to let go. *I relinquished my time in the library to attend the meeting.* —**re•lin•quish•er** n. —**re•lin•quish•ment** n.

re•nounce /rĭ nouns′/ v. **re•nounced, re•nounc•ing, re•nounc•es.** to give up or abandon. *The young prince renounced his claim to the throne.* —**re•nounce•ment** n. —**re•nounc•er** n.

re•press[1] /rĭ prĕs′/ v. **re•pressed, re•press•ing, re•press•es.** to prevent; to hold back; to stop. *The students tried to repress their laughter.*

re•press[2] /rĭ prĕs′/ v. **re•pressed, re•press•ing, re•press•es.** to force from one's mind. *The child tried to repress his fears of the dark.*

re•pres•sive /rĭ prĕs′ ĭv/ adj. causing to prevent, hold back, or stop. *We were greatly delayed by repressive traffic.* —**re•pres•sive•ly** adv. —**re•pres•sive•ness** n.

rep•ri•mand[1] /rĕp′ rə mănd′/ v. **rep•ri•mand•ed, rep•ri•mand•ing, rep•ri•mands.** to scold; to express disapproval. *I thought the teacher should reprimand the giggling students.*

rep•ri•mand[2] /rĕp′ rə mănd′/ n. severe scolding; disapproval. *She received a reprimand for her misbehavior.*

re•sound /rĭ zound′/ v. **re•sound•ed, re•sound•ing, re•sounds.** to ring out or echo loudly. *His voice resounded as he spoke to the crowd.* —**re•sound•ing** adj. —**re•sound•ing•ly** adv.

res•pi•ra•tion /rĕs′ pə rā′ shən/ n. the process of breathing. *Our rate of respiration slows when we are at rest.*

re•sponse /rĭ spŏns′/ n. an answer. *He answered the question with a short response.*

re•sume /rĭ zōōm′/ *v.* **re•sumed, re•sum•ing, re•sumes.** to continue after an interruption. *I will resume the work immediately.* —**re•sum•a•ble** adj.

re•voke /rĭ vōk′/ *v.* **re•voked, re•vok•ing, re•vokes.** to cancel or to put an end to. *Congress voted to revoke the unfair law.*

rit•u•al¹ /rĭch′ ōō əl/ *n.* a ceremony. *The tribe performed a ritual to assure rain.*

rit•u•al² /rĭch′ ōō əl/ *adj.* of or relating to a ceremony. *A cake is a ritual part of birthday celebrations.* —**rit•u•al•ly** adv.

ro•bust¹ /rō bŭst′ or rō′ bŭst′/ *adj.* healthy; strong and vigorous. *He is a robust boy.* —**ro•bust•ly** adv. —**ro•bust•ness** n.

ro•bust² /rō bŭst′ or rō′ bŭst′/ *adj.* rich and full-bodied. *My mother makes chili with a robust flavor.* —**ro•bust•ly** adv. —**ro•bust•ness** n.

rus•tic¹ /rŭs′ tĭk/ *adj.* like or belonging to the country. *The barn and windmill made a rustic scene.*

rus•tic² /rŭs′ tĭk/ *adj.* simple; unsophisticated. *The cabin had a rustic simplicity.*

Ⓢ

sage¹ /sāj/ *adj.* **sag•er, sag•est.** wise. *The professor gave his students sage advice.* —**sage•ly** adv.

sage² /sāj/ *n.* a person with great wisdom. *The medicine man was considered a sage.*

sage³ /sāj/ *n.* a plant that can be used for seasoning. *My grandmother's stuffing is good because she adds sage for flavor.*

sa•van•na or **sa•van•nah** /sə văn′ ə/ *n.* a flat grassland. *Giraffes live on the savannas of Africa.*

sen•sa•tion¹ /sĕn sā′ shən/ *n.* information obtained through one of the five senses. *The sensation of heat made Don move his hand.*

sen•sa•tion² /sĕn sā′ shən/ *n.* a person or thing that causes great excitement. *These books are a sensation among young people.*

sen•si•ble¹ /sĕn′ sə bəl/ *adj.* showing good judgment. *Our plan to arrive home before the storm seemed sensible.* —**sen•si•bly** adv. —**sen•si•ble•ness** n.

sen•si•ble² /sĕn′ sə bəl/ *adj.* that which can be perceived by the senses. *The smell of burnt toast is easily sensible.* —**sen•si•bly** adv. —**sen•si•ble•ness** n.

sen•si•tive¹ /sĕn′ sĭ tĭv/ *adj.* having perception through the senses; easily stimulated. *The eye is sensitive to light.* —**sen•si•tive•ly** adv. —**sen•si•tive•ness** n. —**sen•si•tiv•i•ty** n.

sen•si•tive² /sĕn′ sĭ tĭv/ *adj.* easily hurt or offended. *Because Jane is very sensitive, she is easily hurt.* —**sen•si•tive•ly** adv. —**sen•si•tive•ness** n. —**sen•si•tiv•i•ty** n.

sen•so•ry /sĕn′ sə rē/ *adj.* having to do with the senses. *The smell of bread baking is a wonderful sensory experience.*

so•lar /sō′ lər/ *adj.* related to the sun. *Solar energy is one way to conserve electricity.*

so•lar•i•um /sō lâr′ ē əm/ *n., pl.* **so•lar•i•a** /sō lâr′ ē ə/ or **so•lar•i•ums.** a room or porch surrounded by glass and exposed to the sun. *The solarium is my favorite place to sit.*

sol•stice /sŏl′ stĭs or sōl′ stĭs/ *n.* the twice-yearly occurrence when the sun reaches its farthest north or south point, near June 21 and December 21. *After the winter solstice, the days will begin to get longer.*

staid /stād/ *adj.* having little color or style; without enthusiasm. *Its staid appearance made the house uninviting.* —**staid•ly** adv. —**staid•ness** n.

stam•i•na /stăm′ ə nə/ *n.* the ability to endure. *Joe's stamina remained strong after many hours of exhausting work.*

state•ly /stāt′ lē/ *adj.* **state•li•er, state•li•est.** impressive; grand; with dignity. *The mansion has a stately appearance.* —**state•li•ness** n.

staunch /stônch or stänch/ *adj.* **staunch•er, staunch•est.** devoted; steadfast. *My dog is a staunch companion.* —**staunch•ly** adv. —**staunch•ness** n.

PRONUNCIATION KEY	
/ă/	pat
/ā/	pay
/â/	care
/ä/	father
/är/	far
/ĕ/	pet
/ē/	be
/ĭ/	pit
/ī/	pie
/îr/	pier
/ŏ/	mop
/ō/	toe
/ô/	paw, for
/oi/	noise
/ou/	out
/ōō/	look
/ōō/	boot
/ŭ/	cut
/ûr/	urge
/th/	thin
/th/	this
/hw/	what
/zh/	vision
/ə/	about
	item
	pencil
	gallop
	circus
/ər/	butter

stead•fast /stĕd′ făst/ *adj.* steady; constant. *Her steadfast training helped the team.*
—**stead•fast•ly** *adv.* —**stead•fast•ness** *n.*

strand[1] /strănd/ *v.* **strand•ed, strand•ing, strands.** to leave in a helpless position. *Robinson Crusoe was stranded on an island.*

strand[2] /strănd/ *n.* land that lies along water; beach. *The strand of land was a popular vacation spot.*

strand[3] /strănd/ *n.* one or more threads or fibers that have been twisted or woven together. *The rope contains three strands to make it stronger.*

sub•ter•ra•ne•an /sŭb′ tə rā′ nē ən/ *adj.* beneath the earth's surface; underground. *The men worked in a dangerous subterranean mine.*
—**sub•ter•ra•ne•an•ly** *adv.*

sub•tle[1] /sŭt′ l/ *adj.* **sub•tler, sub•tlest.** small; slight; not obvious. *There is a subtle difference in the color.* —**sub•tly** *adv.*
—**sub•tle•ness** *n.*

sub•tle[2] /sŭt′ l/ *adj.* **sub•tler, sub•tlest.** able to detect small differences. *Jack's subtle hearing helped him tune pianos.*
—**sub•tly** *adv.* —**sub•tle•ness** *n.*

suc•ceed[1] /sək sēd′/ *v.* **suc•ceed•ed, suc•ceed•ing, suc•ceeds.** to do well; to accomplish one's goal. *Our class believed we would succeed.* —**suc•ceed•er** *n.*

suc•ceed[2] /sək sēd′/ *v.* **suc•ceed•ed, suc•ceed•ing, suc•ceeds.** to replace or come after another. *John Adams succeeded George Washington as president.* —**suc•ceed•er** *n.*

sul•len /sŭl′ ən/ *adj.* **sul•len•er, sul•len•est.** sulky; showing ill humor; resentful. *The visitor's sullen attitude made all of us uncomfortable.* —**sul•len•ly** *adv.*
—**sul•len•ness** *n.*

sum•mit[1] /sŭm′ ĭt/ *n.* the highest point; the top. *The climbing team approached the summit of the mountain.*

sum•mit[2] /sŭm′ ĭt/ *n.* a meeting of high level leaders. *The United Nations asked for a summit of the countries' leaders.*

su•per•la•tive[1] /soō pûr′ lə tĭv/ *adj.* superior to all others; highest quality. *Janet's superlative paper deserves a good grade.*
—**su•per•la•tive•ly** *adv.*

su•per•la•tive[2] /soō pûr′ lə tĭv/ *n.* adjective or adverb that is the highest degree. *The superlative of strong is strongest.*

sup•ple /sŭp′ əl/ *adj.* **sup•pler, sup•plest.** moves or bends easily. *The tree's supple branches moved with the wind.* —**sup•ple•ly** *adv.*
—**sup•ple•ness** *n.*

sup•port[1] /sə pôrt′ or sə pōrt′/ *v.* **sup•port•ed, sup•port•ing, sup•ports.** to bear the weight of a structure. *A concrete base supports the structure.*

sup•port[2] /sə pôrt′ or sə pōrt′/ *v.* **sup•port•ed, sup•port•ing, sup•ports.** to favor and act accordingly. *I support my friend's decision.*

sup•port•er /sə pôr′ tər or sə pōr′ tər/ *n.* one who supports and encourages; a follower. *My parents are my best supporters.*

sup•press /sə prĕs′/ *v.* **sup•pressed, sup•press•ing, sup•press•es.** to put an end to; to hold back. *The government suppressed the antiwar demonstration.*

sur•mount /sər mount′/ *v.* **sur•mount•ed, sur•mount•ing, sur•mounts.** to conquer; to overcome. *The athlete surmounted great difficulties to become a winning bicyclist.*
—**sur•mount•er** *n.*

sur•mount•a•ble /sər mount′ ə bəl/ *adj.* able to be conquered or overcome. *A weak defense left their post surmountable.*

sus•tain[1] /sə stān′/ *v.* **sus•tained, sus•tain•ing, sus•tains.** to keep; to maintain. *The musician will sustain the note for a count of four.*
—**sus•tain•a•ble** *adj.* —**sus•tain•er** *n.*
—**sus•tain•ment** *n.*

sus•tain[2] /sə stān′/ *v.* **sus•tained, sus•tain•ing, sus•tains.** to support; to hold up; to keep alive. *Oxygen was used to sustain his breathing in the ambulance.* —**sus•tain•a•ble** *adj.* —**sus•tain•er** *n.* —**sus•tain•ment** *n.*

sus•tain[3] /sə stān′/ *v.* **sus•tained, sus•tain•ing, sus•tains.** to suffer. *Mike sustained an injury in football practice.* —**sus•tain•a•ble** *adj.*
—**sus•tain•er** *n.* —**sus•tain•ment** *n.*

symp•tom /sĭm′ təm or sĭmp′ təm/ *n.* a sign of a disorder or disease. *A fever can be a symptom of illness.* —**symp•to•mat•ic** *adj.*
—**symp•to•mat•i•cal•ly** *adv.*

te•na•cious /tə nā′ shəs/ *adj.* holding firmly to something. *The dog had a tenacious hold on the stick.* —**te•na•cious•ly** *adv.* —**te•na•cious•ness** *n.*

te•nac•i•ty /tə năs′ ĭ tē/ *n.* the state of holding firmly to something. *She stated her belief with tenacity.*

ter•mi•nal[1] /tûr′ mə nəl/ *n.* a mechanical or electrical device in which some type of connection is established. *I do much of my homework at a computer terminal.*

ter•mi•nal[2] /tûr′ mə nəl/ *n.* the station at the end of a transportation line. *The airport is a terminal for many flights.*

ter•mi•nal[3] /tûr′ mə nəl/ *adj.* ending in death; fatal. *His illness is terminal.* —**ter•mi•nal•ly** *adv.*

ter•mi•nate /tûr′ mə nāt′/ *v.* **ter•mi•nat•ed, ter•mi•nat•ing, ter•mi•nates.** to end; to cancel. *We can terminate our contract with the company.* —**ter•mi•na•tion** *n.*

ter•race[1] /tĕr′ ĭs/ *n.* an open, paved area outside a home; a patio. *We enjoyed sitting on the terrace.*

ter•race[2] /tĕr′ ĭs/ *n.* raised earth with sloping sides and a flat top. *Farmers in mountainous areas build terraces to create more farmland.*

ter•rain /tə rān′/ *n.* the features of a particular section of land. *The hilly terrain made building very difficult.*

ter•res•tri•al /tə rĕs′ trē əl/ *adj.* living or growing on land. *Elephants are terrestrial animals.* —**ter•res•tri•al•ly** *adv.* —**ter•res•tri•al•ness** *n.*

ter•ri•to•ry[1] /tĕr′ ĭ tôr′ ē or tĕr′ ĭ tōr′ ē/ *n., pl.* **ter•ri•to•ries.** an area inhabited by a particular animal or animals. *Many birds protect their territory.*

ter•ri•to•ry[2] /tĕr′ ĭ tôr′ ē or tĕr′ ĭ tōr′ ē/ *n., pl.* **ter•ri•to•ries.** a political or geographic region. *The Yukon is a Canadian territory.*

ter•ri•to•ry[3] /tĕr′ ĭ tôr′ ē or tĕr′ ĭ tōr′ ē/ *n., pl.* **ter•ri•to•ries.** the region for which one is directly responsible. *A salesperson was assigned to the new territory.*

tim•id /tĭm′ ĭd/ *adj.* **tim•id•er, tim•id•est.** fearful; shy. *Many wild animals are timid.* —**tim•id•ly** *adv.* —**ti•mid•i•ty** *n.* —**tim•id•ness** *n.*

tra•di•tion /trə dĭsh′ ən/ *n.* an action or a way of behaving that is passed down from previous generations. *It is a tradition to go to my grandma's house on holidays.*

tra•di•tion•al /trə dĭsh′ ə nəl/ *adj.* passed from generation to generation; long-established. *My sister had a traditional Greek wedding.* —**tra•di•tion•al•ly** *adv.*

tran•si•to•ry /trăn′ sĭ tôr ē or trăn′ zĭ tôr′ ē/ *adj.* lasting a short time. *Butterflies have a transitory life.* —**tran•si•to•ri•ly** *adv.* —**tran•si•to•ri•ness** *n.*

trans•lu•cent /trăns lōō′ sənt or trănz lōō′ sənt/ *adj.* letting light through but not transparent. *Frosted glass is translucent.* —**trans•lu•cent•ly** *adv.* —**trans•lu•cence** *n.* —**trans•lu•cen•cy** *n.*

truce /trōōs/ *n.* a temporary halt to a conflict. *The warring countries agreed to a truce.*

ut•ter[1] /ŭt′ ər/ *v.* **ut•tered, ut•ter•ing, ut•ters.** to speak or make a sound. *Do not utter a sound if you want him to be surprised.*

ut•ter[2] /ŭt′ ər/ *adj.* total or complete. *There was utter darkness in the cave.* —**ut•ter•ly** *adv.*

ven•geance /vĕn′ jəns/ *n.* punishment done to another because of an injustice; revenge. *They wanted vengeance for the crime.*

ver•bal•i•za•tion /vûr′ bə lĭ zā′ shən/ *n.* the act of putting thoughts into words. *Verbalization is an important part of communicating ideas.*

ver•bal•ize /vûr′ bə līz′/ *v.* **ver•bal•ized, ver•bal•iz•ing, ver•bal•iz•es.** to put thoughts into words. *Dr. King verbalized the thoughts of many people in his speeches.*

PRONUNCIATION KEY	
/ă/	p**a**t
/ā/	p**a**y
/â/	c**a**re
/ä/	f**a**ther
/är/	f**ar**
/ĕ/	p**e**t
/ē/	b**e**
/ĭ/	p**i**t
/ī/	p**ie**
/îr/	p**ier**
/ŏ/	m**o**p
/ō/	t**oe**
/ô/	p**aw**, f**or**
/oi/	n**oi**se
/ou/	**ou**t
/o͝o/	l**oo**k
/o͞o/	b**oo**t
/ŭ/	c**u**t
/ûr/	**ur**ge
/th/	**th**in
/th/	**th**is
/hw/	**wh**at
/zh/	vi**si**on
/ə/	**a**bout
	item
	penc**i**l
	gall**o**p
	circ**u**s
/ər/	butt**er**

ver•bose /vər bōs'/ *adj.* using more words than needed. *The verbose speaker lost the interest of his audience.* —**ver•bose•ly** *adv.* —**ver•bose•ness** *n.* —**ver•bos•i•ty** *n.*

vi•a•ble /vī' ə bəl/ *adj.* capable of continuing; able to be successful. *The plan is viable if we work hard.* —**vi•a•bil•i•ty** *n.*

vig•or /vĭg' ər/ *n.* strength; physical energy. *The rugby team displayed great vigor during the game.*

vi•sion•ar•y[1] /vĭzh' ə nĕr' ē/ *adj.* having fore-sight. *The visionary planners were prepared for the city's growth.*

vi•sion•ar•y[2] /vĭzh' ə nĕr' ē/ *n., pl.* **vi•sion•ar•ies.** a person with idealistic goals. *The early discoverers were visionaries.*

vi•sion•ar•y[3] /vĭzh' ə nĕr' ē/ *n., pl.* **vi•sion•ar•ies.** a person who has visions or sees apparitions. *The visionary claimed she saw a ghost.*

vo•ca•tion /vō kā' shən/ *n.* a calling for a particular kind of work. *Mary was well-suited for her vocation as a pianist.*

vol•ume /vŏl' yōōm *or* vŏl' yəm/ *n.* loudness. *The volume of the radio was loud enough to shake the house.*

Editorial Development: Cottage Communications

Design and Production: Bill SMITH STUDIO

Cover Illustration: Dave Cutler

Photo and Illustration Credits: Page 6, Hulton-Deutsch Collection/Corbis; 28, Photos.com; 50, Dover; 72, Photos.com; 94, 116, Clipart.com; 138, Corel; 160, Clipart.com; 182, Photos.com

Borders and Icons: Brock Waldron

Context Clues Strategies: Adapted from Camille Blachowicz and Peter J. Fisher. *Teaching Vocabulary in All Classrooms.* (2002). New Jersey: Merrill/Prentice Hall. p. 26

Printed in the United States of America   05 06 07 08 106 5 4 3